The Complete Book of
VSpecial egetarian Delights

◆ COOKING TODAY ◆

Other Titles in the Series by Kamal Mehta

◆ SOUPS, SALADS & DESSERTS

◆ SPECIAL NON-VEGETARIAN DELIGHTS

◆ ALL TIME SNACKS & SANDWICHES

◆ BAKING CAKES & BISCUITS

◆ TIME SAVING HOUSEHOLD HINTS & TIPS

Other Cookery Titles

◆ PARTY SNACKS *Bapsi F. Nariman*

◆ THE COMPLETE BOOK OF
INDIAN PICKLES *Kamal Mehta*

◆ COOKING WITH RICE *Kamal Mehta*

The Complete Book of
Special Vegetarian Delights

Kamal Mehta

HIND POCKET BOOKS

Dedicated in affection to
MY PARENTS
for their love and understanding

THE COMPLETE BOOK OF
SPECIAL VEGETARIAN DELIGHTS
© Kamal Mehta 1993
First paperback edition 1993
ISBN 81-216-0303-X

Published by
HIND POCKET BOOKS PVT. LTD.,
Editorial office: C-36, Connaught Place
New Delhi-110001
H.O.: G.T. Road, Shahdara, Delhi-110032

Designed and typeset at SCANSET
C-36, Connaught Place, New Delhi-110001

Printed at
Rakesh Press, Naraina, New Delhi - 110028

PRINTED IN INDIA

Contents

Foreword
Weights and Measures
Oven Temperatures
Table of Calories
Abbreviations Used
Some Basic Recipes

Dals

Sookhi Dal (*Punjabi*) (*Serves 4-6*)   2

Masur Masala Dal (*Serves 4-6*)   3

Koottu (*Serves 4-6*)   4

Khatti Tur Dal (*Serves 4-6*)   5

Dal Morkuzhambu (*Serves 4-6*)   6

Brinjal Sambar (Kutherakai) (*Tamilian*) (*Serves 4-6*)   8

Khandwi (*Serves 4-6*)   10

Dhoka (*Bengali*) (*Serves 4-6*)   11

Dhokla Special (*Serves 4-6*)   12

Dal Idli   13

Moong Dal Uppuma   14

Moong Dal Dosa   15

Dal-Alu Seekh Kababs (*Serves 4-6*)   16

Dal Fritters (*Serves 4-6*)   17

Dal Gujiya (*Serves 6-8*)   18

Dal Pakoris in Gravy (*Serves 4-6*)   19

Dal Omelette (*Serves 2-3*)   20

Sindhi Dal Palak (*Serves 6-8*)   21

Rajmah (*Serves 4*)   22

Sabat Maanh (*Punjabi*) (*Serves 4-6*)   23

Ghugni (*Serves 2-3*)   24

Dry Kabuli Chana (*Serves 8-10*)   25

Vegetable Dhansak (*Serves 4-6*)   27

Mutton Dhansak (*Serves 4-6*)   28

Chana Dal Gosht *(Serves 8-10)*	29		Masur-Methi Gosht *(Serves 4-6)*	30

Vegetables

Methi Chaman *(Serves 4)*	32		Curried Plantains *(Serves 4-6)*	46
Dum Alu *(Serves 4-6)*	33		Baghara Baingan *(Serves 4-6)*	47
Shahi Stuffed Karelas *(Serves 4-6)*	34		Brinjal-Tomato Bhartha *(Serves 4-6)*	48
Jackfruit Curd Roghan Josh *(Serves 4-6)*	35		Kumra *(Bihari) (Serves 4-6)*	49
Jackfruit Ghanto *(Serves 4-6)*	36		Cottage Cheese Bhaji *(Serves 2-3)*	50
Paneer Makhanae *(Serves 4-6)*	37		Posto Charchari *(Serves 4-6)*	51
Lotus Stem Curry *(Serves 4-6)*	38		Stuffed Capsicums *(Serves 4-6)*	52
Bhein Kofta Curry *(Serves 6-8)*	39		Bhindi Mussalam *(Serves 4-6)*	53
Corn Kofta Curry *(Serves 2-3)*	40		Vegetable Casserole *(Serves 8)*	54
Begumi Cashewnut Curry *(Serves 2-3)*	41		Vegetarian Steamed Mould *(Serves 4-6)*	55
Avial *(Serves 4-6)*	42		Egg-Vegetable Stuffed Cauliflower *(Serves 3-4)*	56
Vegetarian Eggs *(Serves 4-6)*	43		Mince Stuffed Cauliflower *(Serves 3-4)*	57
Potato Potal Dolma *(Serves 4-6)*	45			

Rice

Lemon Rice *(Serves 3-4)*	60		Til Rice *(Serves 3-4)*	65
Tamarind Rice *(Serves 3-4)*	61		Bisi Bele Anna *(South Indian) (Serves 3-4)*	66
Methi Rice *(Serves 3-4)*	62		Coconut Rice *(South Indian) (Serves 3-4)*	67
Dahi Bhaat *(South Indian) (Serves 3-4)*	64		Tomato Rice *(Serves 3-4)*	68

Delicious Vegetable Biryani (*Serves 3-4*)	69
Vegetable Pulao	70
Tahiri (*U.P.*) (*Serves 3-4*)	71
Chana Dal Khichri (*Punjabi*) (*Serves 3-4*)	72
Khichuri (*Bengali*) (*Serves 3-4*)	73
Zafrani Pulao (*Serves 2-3*)	74
Meetha Chawal (*Punjabi*) (*Serves 2-3*)	75
Mutton Biryani (*Serves 3-4*)	76
Yakhni Pulao (*Serves 2-3*)	77
Mutanjan (*Kashmiri*) (*Serves 2-3*)	78
Pastry Pillaf (*Serves 2-3*)	79
Gosht Pulao (*Serves 4-6*)	80
Moti Pulao (*Serves 3-4*)	81
Keema Pulao (*Serves 2-3*)	82
Mince and Rice Casserole (*Serves 3-4*)	83
Chinese Fried Rice (*Serves 3-4*)	84
Chicken Pulao (*Non-Vegetarian*) (*Serves 3-4*)	85

Rotis

Ma-Poli (*Serves 2-3*)	88
Chigri (*Serves 2-3*)	89
Kesari Roti (*Serves 2-3*)	90
Missi Roti (*Serves 2-3*)	91
Missi Makkai ki Roti (*Serves 3-4*)	92
Methi ki Roti (*Serves 2-3*)	93
Chana Dal Roti (*Makes 12 pieces*)	94
Kulcha (*Serves 2-3*)	95
Naan (*Serves 2-3*)	96
Badshahi Naan	97
Bhakhri (*Serves 2-3*)	98
Bati (*Rajasthani*) (*Serves 2*)	98
Kutlame (*Serves 2*)	99
Dogri Bhatura (*Serves 2*)	99
Yeast Bhatura (*Serves 2-3*)	100
Khasta Kachowri (*Serves 2-3*)	101
Thoda (*Serves 2*)	102
Meethi Paronthi (*Serves 2*)	103
Potato Paratha (*Serves 2-3*)	104
Savoury Paratha (*Serves 2-3*)	105
Dal Paratha (*Serves 2-3*)	106
Left-over Dal Paratha (*Serves 2-3*)	107
Paratha with Layers (*Serves 3-4*)	108
Egg Paratha (*Serves 2*)	109
Mince Meat Paratha (*Serves 2-3*)	110

Pickles

Hot Mango Pickle	112	Bhindi Pickle	123
Whole Mango Pickle	113	Brinjal Pickle	124
Mango Pickle (Punjabi)	114	Cucumber Pickle	125
		Onion Pickle (Sindhi)	125
Avakkai	115		
Mango Kutra	116	Tomato Pickle	126
Lime Pickle	116	Turnip Pickle	127
Whole Limes in Salt	117	Mutton Pickle	128
Lemon Pickle	117	Fish Pickle	129
Vegetable Pickle	118	Prawn Pickle	130
Mixed Vegetable Pickle	119	Burmese Balachow I	131
Tamarind Pickle	120	Burmese Balachow II	132
Coriander Pickle	121	Egg Pickle	133
Bamboo Pickle	122	Chicken Pickle	134

Chutneys

Gongura Pachadi	136	Mango Tok	147
Cheena Badam Chutney	136	Sweet Lime Chutney	148
Date Chutney	137	Brinjal Chutney	149
Date and Raisin Chutney	137	Cucumber Chutney	150
Bengal Gram Chutney	138	Green Chilli Chutney	151
Coconut Chutney	139	Mint Chutney	152
Tamarind Chutney	140	Onion Chutney	152
Tamarind-Ginger Chutney	141	Tomato Chutney	153
Ripe Banana Chutney	142	Tomato Tok	154
Gooseberry Chutney	142	Green Tomato and Apple Chutney	155
Mango Chutney	143		
Mango Kasaundi	144	Sweet Tomato Chutney	156
Hot Mango Chutney	145	Tomato-Onion-Mint Chutney	157
Mango Ambal	146		

Glossary   *158*

Common cooking Terms   *166*

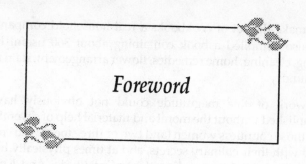

Foreword

This set of 5 cookbooks represents the culmination of over four decades of trial, error and experimentation in the delightful art of cooking. When I arrived in the oil town of Digboi in the extreme north-eastern corner of India, I had just been married and knew little beyond the recipes of my native Punjab. But Digboi brought me into a miniature India with all its tremendous variation in culinary practices and to a society where there were people from all over the world, and a whole new world of cooking opened to me.

With a husband who made no attempt to hide his frank criticism at the dining table and with friends from different cultures and countries, it was not surprising that I started to experiment, innovate and learn new recipes. I have come a long way since then and, it has been great fun. Over the telephone, by writing and in discussions (and after several mistakes) I have gathered what I consider to be the choicest recipes of every national cuisine.

And so the years passed, my daughters grew into womanhood, got married and had children, and like everyone of their generation, they wanted a ready-made solution to this famous art of cooking and eating. To pamper to their whims and fancies and indeed to those of several of their friends and mine, I have undertaken the writing of this book.

These books have over 700 recipes. The names of the spices have been given in Hindi as they are commonly used all over India. A glossary of words and of cooking terms is also included. This will also help the novice in following other cookbooks and in experimenting and innovating on her own. Also included are some "crises" recipes to handle the unexpected but welcome guest.

To make the set of cookbooks a real household companion — I have also compiled a book containing about 360 useful hints on cooking, cleaning, home remedies, flower arrangement, stain removal and laundry.

A work of this magnitude could not obviously have been accomplished without the moral and material help of several people. To all those countless women (and two or three men) who cheerfully parted with their culinary secrets, and at times physically helped in the preparations, I owe a deep debt of gratitude. And I must not forget my husband whose exacting standards in all matters relating to eating have been at once the objective and the attainment of all my endeavours.

Kamal Mehta

Weights and Measures

SOLIDS

1 oz	= 30 gms
2 lbs 2 ozs	= 1 kg
1 tbsp	= 30 gms

LIQUIDS

5-6 ozs	= 1 cup
1 tsp	= 5 ml
1 tbsp	= 20 ml

PULSES

PULSES	1 cup	1 tbsp
Bengal gram	150 gms	
Bengal gram flour	90 gms	
Dry beans	165 gms	
Green gram (whole)	150 gms	
Kabuli chana	150 gms	
Rajmah	150 gms	
Red gram (split)	165 gms	

CEREALS

Cornflour	90 gms	10 gms
Flour (maida)	110 gms	10 gms
Rice	170 gms	20 gms
Sago	140 gms	20 gms
Whole wheat flour (atta)	110 gms	

MILK PRODUCTS

Milk (water)	180 ml	20 ml
Milk $^1/_2$ litre	1 bottle	
Curd	180 gms	30 gms
Cream	200 gms	20 gms
Condensed milk	220 gms	25 gms
Butter	170 gms	20 gms
Khoya	110 gms	15 gms
Cheese (grated)	125 gms	

SUGAR	1 cup	1 tbsp
Sugar	190 gms	20 gms
Castor sugar	160 gms	20 gms
Icing sugar	130 gms	15 gms
Jaggery	200 gms	20 gms

FATS & OILS		
Ghee (melted)	150 gms	12 gms
Ghee (solid)	180 gms	20 gms
Oil	170 gms	10 gms

DRY FRUITS		
Groundnuts (shelled)	120 gms	15 gms
Mixed fruit peel (cut)	120 gms	15 gms
Raisins	120 gms	15 gms
Walnuts (shelled)	120 gms	
Cherries	50 gms	
Dates (seedless) — 10	50 gms	

Oven Temperatures

The recipes state whether the oven should be slow, moderate, hot or very hot, and give the indicative temperature in degrees ^{0}Centigrade as a guide. The actual instructions of the manufacturer should be referred to for further guidance, and adjustments made according to your own experience and results.

	^{0}F ^{0}C	Gas Mark
Very Cool	250^0F = 121^0C	1/4
	275^0F = 135^0C	1/2
Cool	300^0F = 149^0C	1, 2
Warm	325^0F = 163^0C	3
Moderate	350^0F = 177^0C	4
Fairly Hot	375^0F = 191^0C	5
	400^0F = 204^0C	6
Hot	425^0F = 218^0C	7
Very Hot	450^0F = 232^0C	8
	475^0F = 246^0C	9

To convert Fahrenheit into Centigrade: Subtract 32, multiply by 5, then divide by 9. To convert Centigrade into Fahrenheit: Multiply by 9, divide by 5, then add 32.

Table of Calories

	Quantity	Calories
DAIRY PRODUCTS		
Cheese	30 gms	100
Cottage cheese	1 cup	250
Cream	1 tbsp	50
Curd	1 cup	125
Milk (skimmed)	1 cup	80
Milk (whole)	1 cup	150
NUTS		
Almonds	15	100
Cashewnuts	10	100
Coconut fresh	1	110
Groundnuts/peanuts	$1/2$ cup	100
Walnuts	5	100
VEGETABLES		
Beans	$1/2$ cup	90
Beetroot	$1/2$ cup	30
Cabbage	$1/2$ cup	10
Carrot	1	15
Cauliflower	$1/2$ cup	15
Corn	1	70
Cucumber	1 (small)	5
Mushrooms	$1/2$ cup	20
Onion	1	10
Peas	$1/2$ cup	65
Potato (boiled)	1	90
Potato chips	10	115
Spinach	$1/2$ cup	25
Tomato	1	20
Turnips	$1/2$ cup	20
Vegetable soup (clear)	1 cup	80
Vegetable soup (regular)	1 cup	150

FRUITS, CEREALS, PUDDINGS AND FAT

	Quantity	Calories
Apple	1	80
Apple sauce	$^1/_2$ cup	115
Juice	1 cup	150
Peach	1	40
Pear	1	100
Bread slice	1	50
Biscuit	1	80
Pastry	1	250
Rice (boiled)	1 cup	150
Wheat flour	$^1/_2$ cup	200
Pudding/Ice cream	$^1/_2$ cup	150
Vegetable oil	1 tbsp	850

CALORIES USED IN VARIOUS ACTIVITIES PER HOUR

	Calories
Sedentary: reading, writing etc.	100
Light: cooking, dusting, washing etc.	150
Moderate: gardening, sweeping, swabbing	200
Vigorous: brisk walk, golf etc.	300
Strenuous: tennis, running, cycling	350

Abbreviations Used

tsp	teaspoon
tbsp	tablespoon
dsp	dessertspoon
gms	grams
kg	kilogram
ml	millilitre
ltr	litre

Some Basic Recipes

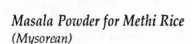

Masala Powder for Methi Rice
(Mysorean)

Fry in very little oil till brown
1 cup Bengal gram dal
1 cup black gram dal

5 cups coriander seeds
60 red chillies
7-cm piece cinnamon

Broil coriander seeds a cup at a time. Broil red chillies and cinnamon. Add to fried dals. Powder well and sieve. Bottle and keep. Use for methi rice or any dals.

Paruppu Pcdy

$^1/_2$ cup arhar dal
$^1/_2$ cup black gram dal
1 tsp pepper
a pinch asafoetida
salt to taste

Roast the two dals separately. Add pepper, asafoetida and salt. Powder and sieve. Store in a bottle. When needed, heat pure ghee, pour on freshly boiled rice and mix in the above powder. Use 2 tsp for each plate.

Canarese Rice Powder

$^1/_2$ cup Bengal gram dal
$^1/_2$ cup green gram dal
$^1/_4$ cup arhar dal
$^1/_4$ cup black gram dal

30 red chillies
15 cloves
10 2-cm pieces cinnamon
$^1/_2$ tsp asafoetida
$^1/_2$ tbsp fenugreek seeds
2 tsp peppercorns
salt to taste

Broil each ingredient separately till golden brown. Powder them separately, add salt to taste, mix well by sieving all together and bottle. Serve with freshly boiled rice and with pure ghee or butter.

Madras Curry Powder

Broil separately
250 gms coriander seeds
60 gms cardamom seeds
250 gms cumin seeds
75 gms peppercorns
100 gms red chillies
75 gms fenugreek seeds
50 gms mustard seeds

20 blades mace
75 gms turmeric powder
100 gms dried ginger

Pound all the ingredients and sieve and bottle.

Curry Powder I

Broil separately
250 gms coriander seeds
25 gms cinnamon
25 gms cardamoms
5 gms cloves
10 gms cumin seeds
1 gm nutmeg
1 gm mace

Powder and pass through a sieve. Store in airtight bottles. Use for any North Indian curry.

Curry Powder II

250 gms coriander seeds
30 gms fenugreek seeds
60 gms cumin seeds
100 gms aniseeds
10 gms cloves
40 gms black cardamoms
20 gms green cardamoms
10 2-cm pieces cinnamon

Broil each ingredient separately on slow fire. Powder, mix and bottle.

Curry Paste

Grind in vinegar
200 gms coriander seeds
25 gms cumin seeds
25 gms turmeric powder
50 gms peppercorns
50 gms mustard seeds
25 gms dry ginger
25 gms garlic
100 gms Bengal gram dal (optional)
10 gms salt
100 gms sugar

1$\frac{1}{4}$ cups white vinegar
1 cup gingelly oil

Heat oil and when it starts smoking, add ground paste and stir-fry till it is done. Cool and bottle.

Don't use any water while grinding. If you want to keep curry paste for a longer time, do not add Bengal gram dal.

Instant Dried Onion Masala

1 kg onions
$\frac{1}{4}$ kg garlic
150 gms ginger

Cut onions, garlic and ginger fine and dry in the sun. When well dried, pound, sieve and bottle. Use to cook any North Indian curry.

Amchoor
(Mango Powder)

1 kg tart mangoes
1 tsp turmeric powder
chilli powder to taste
1 tbsp salt

Peel and slice green mangoes. Apply salt and dry in the sun. After 3 days, rub with chilli and turmeric powders and sun again till thoroughly dry. Pound, sieve and bottle.

Garam Masala

240 gms roasted coriander seeds
20 gms cinnamon
20 gms green cardamoms
20 cloves
15 gms cumin seeds
$1/_2$ nutmeg
10 blades mace

Pound, sieve and bottle.

Kashmiri Garam Masala

2 tbsp black cumin seeds
4 tbsp black cardamoms
1 tbsp peppercorns
2 tsp cloves
1 tbsp cinnamon
10 blades mace
1 nutmeg
6 bay leaves
8 tbsp aniseeds
4 tbsp ginger powder
20 Kashmiri red chillies
4 tbsp coriander seeds

Pound all separately and sieve together. Keep in an airtight bottle.

Dhania – Zeera Masala

5 cups coriander seeds
1 cup cumin seeds
20 red chillies
$^1/_2$ cup fenugreek seeds
$^1/_4$ cup mustard seeds
10 2-cm pieces cinnamon
15 cloves
25 cardamoms
2 nutmegs
15 blades mace
$^1/_4$ cup poppy seeds
8 bay leaves

Broil each separately. Pound, sieve and bottle.

Sambhar Powder I

100 gms Bengal gram dal
200 gms black gram dal
200 gms arhar dal
30 gms peppercorns
30 gms mustard seeds
15 gms fenugreek seeds
30 gms turmeric powder
250 gms red chillies
250 gms coriander seeds
6 sprigs fresh curry leaves
25 gms asafoetida

Broil all ingredients separately. Powder, sieve and bottle.

Sambhar Powder II

$^1/_4$ tsp asafoetida powder
2 tbsp mustard seeds powdered
4 tbsp fenugreek seeds powdered
8 tbsp chilli powder
1 tbsp turmeric powder
2 tbsp table salt
1 tbsp oil

Combine all the powders. Mix in heated and cooled oil and bottle.

Chutney Powder

(Tamilian)

1 cup Bengal gram dal
1 cup arhar dal
50 red chillies
$1/_2$ tsp asafoetida
1 tbsp table salt
a little oil

Broil both dals separately. Fry chillies in a little oil. Remove chillies and in the same oil fry asafoetida. Powder the dals, chillies and asafoetida. Mix with salt and bottle. Serve with idlis and dosas.

Chana Masala

6 tbsp pomegranate seeds
2 tbsp red chillies
1 tsp cloves
1 tsp peppercorns
4 tsp cinnamon
1 tbsp cumin seeds
8 black cardamoms

Pound, sieve and bottle. Use in making Dry Kabuli Chana.

Mint Vinegar

1 cup mint leaves
1 bottle white vinegar

Fill fresh, clean mint leaves loosely in a wide-mouthed bottle and pour in vinegar. Cover and keep for 3 weeks. Strain vinegar and bottle it.

Chilli Vinegar

50 gms small red chillies
1 bottle white vinegar

Procedure is same as above, but filter through a filter paper.

Sour Carom Seeds

500 gms carom seeds
250 gms lemons
20 gms salt

Clean and wash carom seeds and dry in the sun. Meanwhile take out the juice of lemons and add the salt. Soak well-dried carom seeds in juice and keep in the sun till all the juice has been absorbed. Bottle and keep. Good for stomach pain due to wind or gas.

Almond – Mishri Powder

1 kg almonds—shell and grind fine
250 gms sugar-candy—pound fine
25 gms green cardamoms—pound fine

Mix the above ingredients and bottle. Use 1 tsp in a cup of hot milk. It is nutritious and tasty and both adults and children would love it.

Groundnut Pody

Broil separately
4 tbsp Bengal gram dal
4 tbsp black gram dal

1 cup groundnuts — roast and peel
$1/_2$ dry coconut grated
10 red chillies — fry in very little oil
1 cup sesame seeds broiled
1 tsp salt

Pound all the ingredients except salt. Sieve, add salt and bottle. Use for curd dishes or salads.

DALS

Sookhi Dal
(Punjabi)

1 cup black gram dal
1 tbsp ghee
1 tsp cumin seeds
4 green chillies split
salt to taste
2 onions sliced and fried crisp
1 tsp mango powder
$^1/_4$ tsp pepper

Soak black gram dal in water overnight. Rub well, remove skin and drain. Heat ghee, splutter cumin seeds and fry green chillies, add dal and salt and fry for 2-3 minutes. Pour 1½ cups water and cook on high flame till holes appear on top layer. Remove from fire and bake in oven till dal is dry and done (not overcooked).

Put dal on serving dish and garnish with fried brown onions, mango powder and pepper.

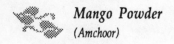

Mango Powder
(Amchoor)

1 kg tart mangoes
1 tsp turmeric powder
1 tbsp salt
chilli powder to taste

Peel and slice green mangoes. Apply salt and dry in the sun. After 3 days, rub with chilli and turmeric powders and sun again till thoroughly dry. Pound, sieve and bottle.

Masur Masala Dal

250 gms masur dal—soak for 15 mins and drain
2 tbsp ghee
salt to taste
1 tsp turmeric powder
3 tomatoes
1 cup curd beaten
$1/_2$ tsp garam masala
coriander leaves

Grind to a paste
2 onions
6 cloves garlic
2 cm piece ginger
4 green chillies

Tarka
2 tsp ghee
$1/_2$ tsp cumin seeds
10 fenugreek seeds

Heat ghee, fry ground paste till ghee floats on top. Add salt, turmeric and tomatoes. Cook again till dry. Add drained dal and enough water to cook it. When half done pour curd and cook again till dal is done. Sprinkle garam masala and cover.

Heat 2 tsp ghee, splutter fenugreek and cumin seeds and pour on top of dal. Garnish with coriander leaves.

Koottu

Boil till soft and mash well
$^1/_2$ cup Bengal gram or moong dal
$^1/_8$ tsp turmeric powder

1 small cabbage shredded
1 potato diced
$^1/_2$ cup peas shelled
few curry leaves
1 tsp sugar
pinch asafoetida
$^1/_2$ tsp mustard seeds
1 tsp black gram dal
2 red chillies

Grind well
3 red chillies
$^1/_2$ coconut grated
$^1/_2$ tsp cumin seeds

Boil vegetables in a little water with salt till done. Add dal, ground masala and curry leaves and boil for a couple of minutes, adding sugar and asafoetida. Take off the fire. Heat oil in pan, splutter mustard, gram and broken chillies and pour over dal. Mix well and serve with chapatis.

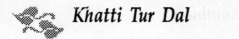

Khatti Tur Dal

Boil till it is like thick soup
1 cup tur/arhar dal
$^1/_4$ tsp turmeric powder
salt to taste
3 cups water

3 tbsp ghee
2 onions sliced
juice of 1 lemon

Grind to a paste
2 cm piece ginger
5 cloves garlic
8 peppercorns
4 cardamoms
2 cm piece cinnamon
1 tsp coriander seeds
1 tsp cumin seeds
1 bunch coriander leaves
4 green chillies

Heat ghee, fry sliced onions till brown. Add masala paste and fry till raw smell disappears. Pour dal soup and cook for five minutes. Mix lemon juice and serve hot with chapatis.

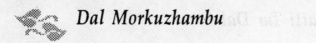

Dal Morkuzhambu

Grind to a coarse paste
1 cup arhar dal
2 red chillies
a pinch asafoetida
salt

Grind to a fine paste, add to
beaten curd mixture
$^1/_2$ coconut
2 red chillies
2 cm piece ginger
1 tsp cumin seeds
$1^1/_2$ tsp coriander seeds
$^1/_2$ tsp pepper
$^1/_4$ tsp fenugreek seeds
3 tsp Bengal gram
salt to taste

Mix well
2 cups sour curd
$1^1/_2$ cups water
1 tbsp oil
$^1/_2$ tsp turmeric powder
a few curry leaves
$^1/_2$ tsp mustard seeds

Tarka
2 tsp oil
$1^1/_2$ tsp mustard seeds
2 red chillies chopped
6 fenugreek seeds
a few coriander leaves

Heat 1 tbsp oil, splutter mustard seeds and curry leaves. Add dal paste and cook for 3-4 minutes. Cool a little and when still warm, make into lemon size balls.

In a saucepan put 1½ cups water and boil. Add balls, salt, turmeric, a few curry leaves and after one boil, pour curd mixture. Simmer for five minutes.

Heat oil, splutter mustard and fenugreek seeds and the chillies and add to Morkuzhambu and garnish with coriander leaves.

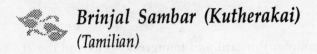

Brinjal Sambar (Kutherakai)
(Tamilian)

Cook on slow fire till dal is done
100 gms arhar dal
$^1/_2$ tsp turmeric powder
1 tsp oil
2 cups water

$^1/_2$ kg brinjals—cut in 5 cm pieces lengthwise
4 tbsp coconut gratings
1 small ball tamarind—squeeze $^1/_2$ cup juice
1 tbsp oil
$^1/_2$ tsp mustard seeds
few curry leaves

Fry in a little oil and powder
4 red chillies
2 tsp fenugreek seeds
$^1/_2$ tsp peppercorns
a pinch asafoetida
1 tbsp Bengal gram dal
2 tbsp coriander seeds
2 cm piece cinnamon
1 tsp cumin seeds

Add brinjals to tamarind juice and the masala powder along with the coconut gratings and a cupful of cold water. Cook till vegetable is done and add to the dal and boil till desired consistency is reached. Take off the fire. Heat oil in a frying pan, splutter mustard seeds and curry leaves. Pour over sambar and serve with rice.

Sambhar Powder I

100 gms Bengal gram dal
200 gms black gram dal
200 gms arhar dal
30 gms peppercorns
30 gms mustard seeds
15 gms fenugreek seeds
30 gms turmeric powder
250 gms red chillies
250 gms coriander seeds
6 sprigs fresh curry leaves
25 gms asafoetida

Broil all ingredients separately. Powder, sieve and bottle.

Sambhar Powder II

¼ tsp asafoetida powder
2 tbsp mustard powder
4 tbsp fenugreek powder
8 tbsp chilli powder
1 tbsp turmeric powder
2 tbsp table salt
1 tbsp oil

Combine all the powders. Mix in heated and cooled oil and bottle.

Khandwi

Mix well with 2 cups water till no lumps remain
2 cups Bengal gram flour
2 cups sour curd
1 tsp green chilli paste
1 tsp ginger paste
salt to taste
$^1/_2$ tsp turmeric powder

2 tbsp til oil
1 tsp mustard seeds
3 tsp coriander leaves
1 tbsp grated coconut

Cook liquid in a pan till raw smell disappears. Take off the fire and pour a thin layer into a flat thal. When cool and dry, cut into strips and roll.

Garnish : Heat oil, splutter mustard seeds. Pour over rolls which have been kept in serving dish, top with grated coconut and coriander leaves.

Dhoka
(Bengali)

1 cup Bengal gram dal—soak overnight,
  drain and grind to a paste

Grind and mix with dal paste
1 onion
2 cm piece ginger
$^1/_2$ tsp cumin seeds
6 green chillies
salt to taste

ghee for frying
2 onions sliced
1 tsp cumin seed powder
$^1/_2$ tsp chilli powder
1 tsp turmeric powder
2 tomatoes chopped
2 potatoes—peel, cut in cubes and fry golden brown
salt to taste
1 tsp sugar
$^1/_2$ tsp garam masala

Heat 1 tbsp ghee and add dal paste mixed with masalas. Cook till moisture is absorbed. In an oiled tray spread dal mixture 2 cm thick and level it with your hand. Cool and cut in 2 cm pieces (cubes) and deep fry till golden brown.

In another pan, put 2 tbsp ghee, fry the sliced onions, the powder masalas and the chopped tomatoes till masala is ready. Add sugar, salt, the fried potatoes and a cupful of water to cook the curry. When a little gravy remains, add dal cubes. Sprinkle with garam masala and cook for 3 minutes.

Dhokla Special

Grind to a paste
250 gms Bengal gram—soak overnight and drain
6 green chillies
2 cm piece ginger
2 cm piece turmeric
small bunch coriander leaves
$\frac{1}{2}$ tsp chilli powder
a pinch asafoetida
8 peppercorns
$\frac{1}{4}$ coconut

salt to taste
ghee for frying

Spread paste on a greased thali and steam till it comes off the thali. Cut in 5 cm × 2 cm pieces and cool. Deep fry and serve hot with mint chutney.

Variation
Grind to a paste
1 cup masur dal—soak overnight and drain
1 cup rice—soak overnight and drain
2 cm piece ginger
3 green chillies

salt to taste
$\frac{1}{4}$ cup curd
pinch soda-bi-carb

Mix paste with salt, beaten curd and soda, add a little water and beat well. Pour into small oiled katoris and steam till done. Serve with any pickle.

Dal Idli

1 cup moong dal washed—soak and grind to a rough paste
1 cup urad dal washed—soak and grind to a fine paste
salt to taste
1 tsp ginger paste
6 green chillies ground

Mix dals with ginger and chillies and keep overnight in a warm place (10-12 hrs). Stir mixture well adding salt and a little water to make heavy dropping consistency. Steam in an idli cooker or katoris and serve with chutney.

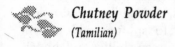

Chutney Powder
(Tamilian)

1 cup Bengal gram dal
1 cup arhar dal
50 red chillies
½ tsp asafoetida
1 tbsp table salt
a little oil

Broil both dals separately. Fry chillies in a little oil. Remove chillies and in the same oil fry asafoetida. Powder the dals, chillies and asafoetida. Mix with salt and bottle. Serve with idlis and dosas.

Moong Dal Uppuma

1 kg whole green gram
750 gms potatoes
1 tsp mustard seeds
1 tbsp oil
1 tsp cumin seeds
a few curry leaves
a pinch asafoetida
4 red chillies broken
4 green chillies chopped
2 cm piece ginger chopped
juice of 2 limes
salt to taste

Soak green gram overnight. Drain and tie in muslin bag till sprouted. Semi-boil potatoes, peel and grate finely. Heat oil, add mustard and cumin seeds, red chillies, asafoetida and cury leaves. When they start to splutter add grated potatoes, sprouted green gram, salt, green chillies and ginger and cook till done. Add lime juice, mix and serve hot.

Note : In winter gram takes longer to sprout so soak it 24 hrs. ahead. After 8 hrs. of soaking tie it in a muslim bag, it will take another 16 hrs. to sprout.

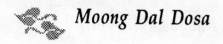

Moong Dal Dosa

250 gms green gram dal—soak
    and grind into a soft paste
a pinch asafoetida
salt to taste
oil for frying

Chop fine
3 green chillies
2 onions
few coriander leaves

Mix dal paste with asafoetida, salt and chopped ingredients.

Heat a griddle and grease it, spread a big ladleful on it and cook on slow fire adding drops of ghee on the sides. When one side is done turn and brown the other side also. Serve with coconut chutney.

Dal-Alu Seekh Kababs

225 gms potatoes—boil and mash
salt to taste
mango powder
oil for frying

Grind to a paste
1 cup black gram dal—soak and drain
6 cloves garlic
2 cm piece ginger
small bunch coriander leaves
8 green chillies

Mix paste with mashed potatoes and salt. Divide them into 25 small balls. Take a wooden stick ½ cm thick, grease it and wrap the ball around it with greased fingers. Gently remove it and deep fry till light brown. Fry all the kababs like this. Sprinkle mango powder or chaat masala (available in packets) on hot kababs and serve.

Note : Do not add any water while grinding dal.

Dal Fritters

Soak overnight and grind
5 tbsp Bengal gram dal
4 tbsp arhar dal
2 tbsp masur dal

2 onions chopped fine
4 green chillies chopped fine
1 bunch coriander leaves chopped
2 tbsp cottage cheese
2 tsp coriander powder
1 tsp chilli powder
salt to taste
oil for deep frying

Mix the ground ingredients with the other ingredients and beat well using a little water, if necessary, to make a thick batter, sufficient to remain unmoved in a spoon. Heat oil and when smoking hot, drop spoonfuls of batter and fry fritters till crisp and light brown. Serve hot with any chutney.

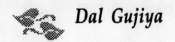

Dal Gujiya

800 gms thick curd
salt
oil for frying

Grind to a fine paste and beat well
250 gms urad dal—soak for 1 hr
6 green chillies
2 cm piece ginger

Chop fine for filling and mix with
the next two ingredients
25 raisins
a few mint leaves
6 green chillies
8 cashewnuts

1 tsp coriander powder
$^1/_4$ tsp garam masala

Garnish
2 tsp roasted cumin seed powder
6 red chillies
a little black salt
chopped green coriander

Beat dal paste well, adding a little salt. Take a muslin cloth, spread it on a wooden board and wet it. Take one tablespoonful of dal batter, spread it like a cutlet and put a tsp of filling on one half, with the help of the muslin, fold the other half over and slide it in the oil. Let it fry evenly on both sides, drain and cool. Then drop in cold water. Do the same till the entire batter is used up. Keep in cold water for ½ hour, then squeeze them out (pressing them between the palms of your hands without breaking them) and lay them on a rice platter. Pour the beaten curd on top to cover them fully.

Garnish with roasted powders, black salt and chopped coriander.

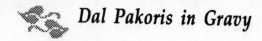

Dal Pakoris in Gravy

Make a thick batter and keep for 25 mins
1 cup Bengal gram flour
1 tbsp ghee
$\frac{1}{2}$ tsp chilli powder
$\frac{3}{4}$ tsp cumin seeds
$1\frac{1}{2}$ tsp coriander powder
$\frac{1}{4}$ tsp soda-bi-carb
salt to taste
a few coriander leaves chopped

Grind to a paste for gravy
3 onions
6 cloves garlic

ghee for frying
2 tomatoes chopped fine
$\frac{1}{2}$ tsp chilli powder
1 tsp turmeric powder
$\frac{1}{2}$ tsp garam masala
1 tsp coriander powder
a little salt for gravy
2 cups water
coriander leaves chopped

Heat ghee, fry small pakoris made with the batter, drain and keep aside.

In 1 tbsp ghee, fry ground garlic-onion paste. When golden brown add turmeric and chilli powders and chopped tomatoes. Cook till ghee separates. Add remaining masalas and salt, pour 2 cups water and cook till half the liquid evaporates. Add pakoris and cook for five minutes only. Serve hot, garnished with coriander leaves.

Note : If kept too long after cooking the pakoris soak up all the gravy and break easily.

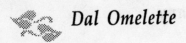

Dal Omelette

2 tbsp masur dal
3 eggs beaten
salt and pepper to taste
2 tbsp ghee
little tomato sauce

Chop
1 onion
a few coriander leaves
3 green chillies

Cook dal in a little water and make a paste. To the eggs add dal paste, seasoning and the chopped ingredients and mix well. In a frying pan, heat oil, pour the mixture and slowly cook. When one side is set, spread tomato sauce, roll like an omelette and cook for one minute more. Serve immediately.

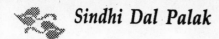

Sindhi Dal Palak

$^1/_2$ kg palak—wash and chop
$^3/_4$ cup Bengal gram dal—soak for $^1/_2$ an hr
2 tbsp ghee
1 tsp turmeric powder
1 tsp coriander powder
2 green chillies chopped
salt to taste

Chop fine
2 onions
5 cm piece ginger
250 gms tomatoes
1 small brinjal
1 carrot
100 gms squash or bottle gourd
1 potato
a small bunch fenugreek leaves
a small bunch soa saag

Heat ghee and lightly fry the onions, then add all other ingredients except Bengal gram dal. Stir to mix well, adding ½ cup of water. Lastly add the dal and simmer on slow fire till well cooked (approx. 1½ hrs). Do not stir after adding dal. Mash well, to consistency of thick cream, before serving.

Rajmah

Soak overnight and boil till soft
500 gms kidney beans (rajmah)
1 bay leaf

2 tbsp butter
2 tbsp flour
1$\frac{1}{2}$ cups milk
1 cup tomato puree
1 onion chopped very fine
1 tbsp sugar
$\frac{1}{4}$ cup treacle (made from jaggery)
salt to taste
1 tsp fat

Drain beans. Retain liquid and discard bay leaf. Heat butter, fry chopped onion till it changes its colour, brown flour and add milk, stirring all the time for 3 minutes. Add tomato puree, salt, the liquid from the beans, sugar and treacle and cook till half the liquid dries up. In a fire-proof dish, melt 1 tsp fat, pour the beans mixed with the cooked sauce. Cover and bake slowly for an hour till the beans are pleasantly moist and no liquid remains.

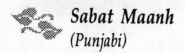

Sabat Maanh
(Punjabi)

Wash and drain
1/2 kg whole black dal
50 gms Bengal gram dal

2 tbsp oil
salt to taste
6 Kashmiri chillies
2 pods garlic chopped fine
2 onions chopped fine

Tarka
4 tbsp ghee
a pinch asafoetida
2 onions sliced
5 cm piece ginger cut in matchsticks
1/2 tsp chilli powder
1 tsp cumin seeds
1 tsp garam masala
2 cups curd

In a heavy bottomed pan heat 10 cups water. As it boils add dals and let cook on medium flame (maintain same temperature throughout) till dal grains burst. Add 2 tbsp oil, salt, Kashmiri chillies, chopped garlic and onions and let simmer on slow fire (adding hot water if necessary) for 2 hrs. or more, till dal is well cooked and becomes reddish in colour. Heat ghee, fry asafoetida and mash. Add onions and when half-fried, add ginger pieces and fry till brown. Add cumin seeds, chilli powder, garam masala and whipped curd and cook till ghee separates. Add dal and cook again for 5 minutes.

Serve with whipped cream or home-made butter. This is optional.

Ghugni

250 gms dried peas—soak overnight
150 gms potatoes—peel and cut in 2 cm cubes
3 cm piece ginger—chop fine
2 tbsp coconut—cut in $\frac{1}{2}$ cm cubes
2 tsp chilli powder
salt to taste
2 tbsp cumin seeds—roast and powder
2 balls tamarind (lemon size)—strain $\frac{1}{2}$ cup juice
1 tbsp sugar

Boil soaked peas in plenty of water on slow fire till nearly done. Add potato cubes, ginger, coconut and salt and cook till peas and potatoes are absolutely soft but not overdone. Sprinkle cumin seed and chilli powders and salt and cook for another five minutes. Take off the fire, add strained tamarind juice and sugar. Mix well and serve. To make more pungent, add more chilli powder.

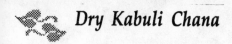

Dry Kabuli Chana

500 gms Kabuli chana—wash and soak overnight
1 tsp soda-bi-carb
2 tsp tea leaves tied in a muslin bag
6 potatoes cut in fingers
5 cm piece ginger cut in long thin slices
3 tbsp roasted coriander seed powder
2 tbsp roasted cumin seed powder
2 tsp chilli powder
2 tbsp pomegranate seeds or
mango powder
2 tsp garam masala
salt to taste
1 cup ghee
small bunch coriander leaves chopped
8 green chillies
2 onions chopped

Boil chanas with tea-bag and soda-bi-carb in plenty of water on slow fire, till they become tender and water nearly dries up. Discard tea-bag. Fry potato fingers till soft and golden brown. Drain and keep aside. Sprinkle all the masalas and salt on the chanas and toss well. Heat ghee. When smoking hot, fry the ginger pieces golden brown and pour over chanas. Mix well. Add fried potato fingers and mix. Keep on a very slow fire for 30-40 minutes tossing occasionally. Serve when absolutely dry. Garnish with chopped coriander, green chillies and chopped onions.

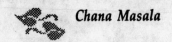

Chana Masala

6 tbsp pomegranate seeds
2 tbsp red chillies
1 tsp cloves
1 tsp peppercorns
4 tsp cinnamon
1 tbsp cumin seeds
8 black cardamoms

Pound, sieve and bottle. Use in making Dry Kabuli Chana.

Vegetable Dhansak

Pick, wash, and soak for 10 mins I
150 gms arhar dal
25 gms masur dal
25 gms moong dal
25 gms chana dal

Broil and powder II
4 red chillies
1 tsp cumin seeds
1 tbsp dry coconut

Chop fine III
2 cm piece ginger
6 cloves garlic
small bunch coriander leaves
10 mint leaves
3 green chillies
small bunch fenugreek leaves

Cut in pieces IV
1 slice red pumpkin
2 potatoes
2 brinjals

3 red tomatoes chopped
2 onions chopped
1 tbsp ghee
$1/2$ tsp garam masala
1 tsp sambar powder
salt to taste

Cook I, II, III, IV, all mixed together in a pan with enough water. When dal is cooked add chopped tomatoes and salt. Mash well and sieve through a strainer.

Heat 1 tbsp ghee, fry chopped onions, add garam masala and sambar powder. Pour dal liquid over it and cook for 2 minutes. Serve with brown rice.

Mutton Dhansak

Wash and soak for 20 mins, drain
120 gms arhar dal
60 gms masur dal
60 gms moong dal

Grind to a paste I
1 tsp turmeric powder
1 onion
4 green chillies
5 cloves garlic

Cut in pieces
1 brinjal
1 large potato
1 small slice red pumpkin

$^1/_2$ kg mutton pieces
salt to taste
2 tbsp ghee
3 tomatoes chopped
3 onions sliced
1 tbsp green coriander chopped
$^1/_2$ tsp garam masala

Grind to a paste II
$^1/_2$ tsp fenugreek seeds
$^1/_2$ tsp mustard seeds
1 tsp chilli powder
2 tsp coriander seeds
1 tsp cumin seeds
1 tbsp tamarind juice

Place dals, mutton, and cut vegetables in a pan with salt and ground paste I, and enough water to cook the dals and mutton.

In 2 tbsp ghee fry onions, ground paste II and the chopped tomatoes. Remove mutton pieces from dal and keep aside. With an egg beater beat the dal well and pour over fried masala adding chopped coriander. Add mutton pieces and put on slow fire for 5 minutes. Sprinkle ½ tsp garam masala and serve with brown rice.

Chana Dal Gosht

1 kg mutton cut in small pieces
$^1/_2$ kg Bengal gram dal
1 bay leaf
2 onions chopped
1 pod garlic chopped
1 tsp turmeric powder
salt to taste
100 gms ghee for frying and cooking
2 onions sliced
5 green chillies split
1 tsp cumin seeds
1 tsp chilli powder

Boil mutton along with bay leaf, chopped onions, ginger, garlic and a little salt till it is nearly done. Remove mutton pieces and strain juice mashing the garlic and ginger well. Throw away the residue. In the same juice pour more water to make 6 cups, add washed and strained dal, turmeric powder and salt to taste. Let cook on slow fire till half done. Fry mutton pieces till light brown and add them to dal. Cook them till dal is tender and proper consistency obtained. Take off the fire.

Heat ghee in a frying pan, brown sliced onions and split green chillies. Splutter cumin seeds and add chilli powder and pour over cooked dal. Serve with parathas or boiled rice.

Note : Best cooked in an earthenware pot on a very slow fire.

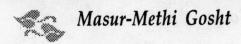

Masur-Methi Gosht

250 gms mutton—cut in small pieces and boil well
1 coconut—extract 1 cup thick and 1 cup thin milk
1 cup masur dal—wash and soak for 15 mins
salt to taste
2 bunches fenugreek leaves—pluck leaves only

Grind
3 green chillies
8 flakes garlic
1 small bunch coriander leaves
8 mint leaves
6 peppercorns
8 red chillies
1 tbsp cumin seeds
1 tsp mustard seeds
2 cm piece turmeric

2 tbsp ghee
3 onions sliced
juice of 1 lime

Cook dal with fenugreek leaves, salt, 1 cup thin coconut milk and 1 cup water, till well done. Heat ghee in another pan, fry onions brown, add ground paste and fry for further 5 minutes. Add dal mixture, salt and boiled mutton pieces and simmer on a very slow fire. When nearly done, add first milk of coconut and juice of one lime. Garnish with chopped coriander.

VEGETABLES

Methi Chaman

Grind
250 gms spinach
125 gms fenugreek leaves

200 gms potato fingers
150 gms cottage cheese cubes
4 tbsp ghee
1 cup butter-milk slightly sour
salt to taste
1 tsp turmeric powder
1 tbsp coriander powder
1 tsp red chilli powder
1 tsp Kashmiri garam masala

Heat ghee, fry cottage cheese cubes golden brown and drain. Fry potato fingers also golden and drain. In the same ghee add ground greens and fry till ghee separates, add half the butter-milk, salt, turmeric, coriander and chilli powders, potato fingers, fried cottage cheese cubes. Simmer on slow fire till fingers are soft and add rest of the butter-milk and cook till ghee separates from curry. Sprinkle 1 tsp Kashmiri garam masala.

Serve with boiled rice.

Dum Alu

$^1/_2$ kg potatoes

Roast and powder
4 black cardamoms
2 cm stick cinnamon
1 tsp black cumin seeds
1 tsp cumin seeds
3 cloves
6 peppercorns
2 tsp coriander seeds
2 cm piece turmeric

Grind to a paste
2 onions
1 pod garlic

ghee for frying
1 bay leaf
$^1/_4$ tsp asafoetida
1 cup curd
salt for gravy
$^1/_2$ tsp garam masala
1 tbsp coriander leaves chopped

Boil potatoes, peel and slice off the tops. Scoop out hollows and keep lids along with respective potatoes. Take half the powders and mash up with potato scoops and fill in the hollows. Put lids back and secure with toothpicks. Deep fry till dark brown. Drain.

Heat 2 tbsp ghee, fry bay leaf, asafoetida and onion-garlic paste. Fry till brown. Add a little salt and the balance of the powders and the beaten curd. Cook till ghee separates. Add garam masala and half a cup of water. Give one boil and lay the stuffed potatoes carefully and cook for 5 minutes on slow fire till gravy is thick. Sprinkle with chopped coriander leaves.

Shahi Stuffed Karelas

$^1/_2$ kg green, large bitter gourds
1 tsp turmeric powder
2 tsp salt

Mix together
3 potatoes—peel and grate
$^1/_2$ tsp chilli powder
salt to taste
4 tsp coriander powder
1 tsp garam masala
$^1/_2$ tsp turmeric powder

thread for tying
ghee for frying
2 tbsp ghee for cooking
3 onions chopped
salt to taste
$^1/_2$ tsp turmeric powder
$^1/_2$ tsp chilli powder
1 tbsp coriander powder
$^1/_2$ tsp cumin seed powder
$^1/_4$ kg tomatoes chopped
$^1/_2$ cup curd
salt

With a blunt knife scrape the bitter gourds from outside. Slit them and apply turmeric and salt well, inside and outside and marinate for 2 hours. Wash well under running water and squeeze out all the water. Fill the bitter gourds with potato mixture and tie each one with thread.

Heat ghee and fry them on slow fire till brown. Drain and keep aside.

In another pan, heat 2 tbsp ghee, fry chopped onions brown. Add masala powders, salt, chopped tomatoes and curd till tomatoes are pulpy. Add fried bitter gourds and cook on slow fire for another 10 minutes.

Note: Cooked mince meat can be stuffed instead of potatoes.

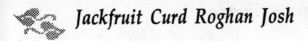

Jackfruit Curd Roghan Josh

1 kg jackfruit
1 tsp turmeric powder
1 tsp salt
ghee for frying

Grind to a paste
2 big onions
1 pod garlic

1 tbsp ginger water
1 cup curd
1 tsp garam masala
1 tbsp roasted coriander seed powder
salt to taste
1 tsp chilli powder
1 tsp turmeric powder

Peel and cut the jackfruit in 3 cm pieces and boil in 2 cups of water with 1 tsp each of turmeric and salt for 10 minutes. Drain away the water and cool the pieces. Heat ghee and fry the boiled pieces brown, a few at a time, keep aside. Drain ghee also to remove any fried pieces of jackfruit. Take 3 tbsp ghee and fry ground paste sprinkling ginger-water at intervals, add turmeric and chilli powders and fry till masala is brown. Pour beaten curd and cook till water dries up and ghee separates. Add coriander powder, garam masala, 1 cup water, fried jackfruit pieces and mix well. Put the lid on the pan and let simmer for 5 minutes. Sprinkle garam masala and serve with chapatis.

Jackfruit Ghanto

$^1/_2$ kg raw jackfruit
1 tsp turmeric powder
4 tbsp mustard oil
1 cup potato cubes
1 tsp pure ghee
$^1/_4$ tsp nigella seeds
2 bay leaves
4 green chillies slit
6 cardamoms
2 cloves
5 cm stick cinnamon
2 cm piece ginger ground
2 tsp turmeric powder
$^1/_2$ cup milk
$1^1/_2$ tsp sugar
salt to taste
$^1/_4$ coconut
$^1/_2$ tsp garam masala

Grind

2 tsp aniseeds
1 tsp coriander seeds
1 tsp cumin seeds

Peel and cut jackfruit into 1 cm pieces and soak in 1 cup of water with turmeric powder for 15 minutes, then boil and drain them. Heat mustard oil, fry potato cubes till hard but not brown, drain and keep aside. To same oil add pure ghee and heat. Add nigella seeds, bay leaves, green chillies, cloves, cardamoms, broken cinnamon and aniseed paste and fry for 2 minutes. Add turmeric, ground ginger and fry a little adding milk, sugar, salt and also the grated coconut. Mix well and cook till milk is half absorbed. Add boiled jackfruit, cover and cook on very slow fire for 15 minutes. When half done, add fried potato cubes and cook till potatoes and jackfruit are fully done. Put in serving dish.

Optional: Heat a tablespoon of ghee and powdered garam masala and give final tarka for additional flavour.

Paneer Makhanae

250 gms cottage cheese
4 level tbsp flour or arrowroot
salt to taste
$\frac{1}{2}$ tsp garam masala
a pinch soda-bi-carb

Filling
1 tbsp walnuts chopped
1 tbsp cashewnuts chopped
1 tbsp coriander leaves chopped
1 tsp mint chopped

Grind to a paste for gravy
3 onions
1 pod garlic
2 cm piece ginger
6 green chillies

2 ripe tomatoes chopped
1 cup curd whipped
1 tbsp roasted coriander seed powder
1 bunch coriander leaves chopped
salt to taste
ghee for frying
100 gms puffed lotus seeds

Mash cottage cheese, flour, salt, garam masala and a pinch of soda-bi-carb with the ball of your hand for 8-10 minutes till smooth. Form into marble-size balls after filling with nut mixture. Deep fry golden brown and drain.

Fry lotus seeds, drain and keep aside. Make gravy like Jackfruit Curd Rogan Josh. Pour water for gravy and boil till ready, adding fried lotus seeds a few minutes before taking off the fire. Arrange cottage cheese balls in the serving dish, pour gravy and serve immediately.

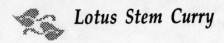

Lotus Stem Curry

$^1/_2$ kg thick lotus stems

Make batter
1 tbsp flour
4 tbsp water
1 pinch salt

Mix with very little water
1 tbsp coriander powder
1 tbsp mango powder
$^1/_2$ tsp chilli powder
$^1/_2$ tsp cumin seed powder
$^1/_4$ tsp garam masala
salt to taste

1 cup sour curd whipped
1 tsp sugar
salt and chilli powder to taste
5 tbsp ghee

Cut lotus stems 3 cm long. Wash well under tap water to remove any mud that may be there and drain well. Fill holes with masala, dip open sides in flour batter and fry on very slow fire to soften and brown them. This takes about 20-25 minutes. Whip curd, add a tsp sugar and pour on top adding the remaining masala, salt and chilli powder and cook till dry. Add half a cup of water and cook to make a little gravy.

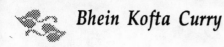

Bhein Kofta Curry

250 gms lotus stems—cut in pieces and boil

Grind to a paste
1 onion
3 flakes garlic
2 cm piece ginger

3 tbsp gram flour
$\frac{1}{2}$ tsp chilli powder
salt to taste
$\frac{1}{4}$ tsp garam masala
$\frac{1}{4}$ tsp roasted cumin seed powder
oil for frying

For gravy
2 tbsp ghee
2 onions
1 pod garlic
2 tomatoes or $\frac{1}{2}$ cup curd
2 tsp coriander powder
little salt
1 tsp turmeric powder
$\frac{1}{2}$ tsp chilli powder
$\frac{1}{4}$ tsp garam masala
1 tbsp coriander leaves chopped

Grind boiled lotus stems fine and add to ground paste. Mix gram flour, chilli powder, salt, garam masala and cumin seed powder. Mix well. Form into marble-size balls and deep fry in hot oil or ghee till golden brown. Drain and keep.

Curry : Grind onions and garlic and fry in 2 tbsp ghee till light golden. Add chopped tomatoes or curd, salt, turmeric, chilli and coriander powders and fry till ghee separates. Add 2 cups water and simmer gravy for 10 minutes. Add fried koftas and cook for another 10 minutes. Sprinkle garam masala and serve hot garnished with chopped coriander.

Variation : Can be made with bottle gourd and green plantains instead of lotus stems.

Corn Kofta Curry

6 corn cobs
50 gms gram flour
200 gms ghee
1 large onion
1 tbsp peanut powder
2 tbsp coconut grated
3 green chillies
1 tbsp red chilli powder
1 tsp turmeric powder
1 tbsp cumin seeds
2 ripe tomatoes
$\frac{1}{2}$ cup curd
$\frac{1}{2}$ tbsp mustard seeds
1 tbsp ginger and garlic paste
salt and pepper to taste
1 tbsp coriander leaves chopped

Grate corn, chop onion and green chillies fine. Prepare stiff batter mixing gram flour, grated coconut, onion and green chillies, salt and grated corn. Make small balls and fry on slow fire till golden brown.

In a separate pan heat a little ghee, add mustard seeds, then the rest of the masalas and then peanut powder and curd and fry a while. Add chopped tomatoes, water and salt. Add koftas a few at a time to the boiling gravy. When gravy is thick, garnish with coriander leaves and pepper. Serve hot.

Begumi Cashewnut Curry

200 gms cashewnuts
1 cup milk
2 tbsp ghee
6 cardamoms
6 cloves
5 cm stick cinnamon
1 bay leaf
1 tsp cumin seeds
1 tsp chilli powder
salt to taste
1 cup curd
1 cup solidified milk (khoa)
$\frac{1}{2}$ tsp garam masala
1 tsp sugar

Wash cashewnuts and soak them in 1 cup milk for 20 minutes.

Heat ghee, fry cloves, cinnamon, cardamoms, cumin seeds and bay leaf. Add chilli powder, salt and beaten curd in which 1 tsp sugar has been mixed and cook till half the liquid dries up. Add cashewnuts, solidified milk, and garam masala and half cup water. Cook till ghee separates. Sprinkle garam masala.

Note : Do not make and keep it for long as cashewnuts tend to become soggy. Cook a few minutes before serving.

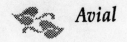

Avial

100 gms potatoes
1 raw banana
2 drumsticks
50 gms beans
50 gms carrots
100 gms brinjals
50 gms cabbage
1 cup thick, sour curd
1 tsp turmeric powder
salt to taste
$^1/_2$ tsp chilli powder
1 sprig curry leaves
1 tbsp coconut oil

Grind coarsely
$^1/_2$ coconut grated
1 tsp cumin seeds
4 green chillies

Wash, peel and cut vegetables into long pieces. Cook in 2 cups of water with turmeric, chilli powder and salt. Combine curd and ground paste and add when vegetables are well cooked. Bring to boil. Add coconut oil and curry leaves and serve.

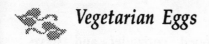

Vegetarian Eggs

Mash well
50 gms processed cheese
2 tbsp cottage cheese (made from dripped curd)
1 drop orange colouring

Mix well
$^1/_2$ kg potatoes boiled and mashed
1 tsp cornflour
salt to taste
$^1/_4$ tsp garam masala
$^1/_2$ tsp chilli powder

ghee for frying
2 tbsp ghee
4 cardamoms
2 cloves
$^1/_2$ tsp cumin seeds
2 big onions chopped
6 flakes garlic chopped
$^1/_2$ tsp turmeric powder
$^1/_2$ tsp chilli powder
2 tbsp tomato puree or $^1/_2$ cup thick curd
250 gms solidified milk (khoa)
salt to taste

Mash cheese mixture well and form into yolk size balls. Divide potato mixture into the number of yolks made. Flatten each piece, fill with yolk, roll into ball and deep fry, till all pieces are golden brown.

In a heavy bottomed pan, put 2 tbsp ghee, chopped garlic and onion and fry till pale brown. Add whole masalas and brown till onions are golden brown. Add turmeric, chilli and salt and the beaten curd (or tomato puree) and cook till ghee separates from masala. Add powdered, solidified milk and fry again. Pour in a cupful of water and boil for a few minutes. Carefully, lay down the 'Eggs' and simmer for five minutes. Garnish with chopped coriander and serve immediately.

Note : The gravy can be made and kept well ahead and served when needed.

Potato Potal Dolma

250 gms pointed gourd
100 gms potato cubes fried
100 gms cottage cheese

Grind to a paste
2 cm piece ginger
4 green chillies
1 tsp coriander seeds
$^1/_2$ tsp cumin seeds
salt to taste

Mix and make batter
1 tbsp flour
4 tbsp water
pinch salt

Gravy
2 onions sliced
1 cm piece ginger chopped
1 tsp turmeric powder
4 cardamoms
2 cm stick cinnamon
2 cloves
2 bay leaves
$^1/_2$ tsp chilli powder
$^1/_2$ tsp cumin seed powder
1 tsp coriander powder
1 cup curd
salt to taste
1 tsp sugar
3 tbsp ghee

Soak gourd in water, scrape lightly, give one gentle boil and cool. Slit tops, scoop out seeds and pulp, stuff cheese and ground paste. Close opening with a little flour batter and deep fry till light brown. Heat ghee, fry bay leaves, cloves, cardamoms and cinnamon. Add sliced onions and fry till brown, add ginger, all the powders, curd, sugar and salt and fry till ghee separates. Add fried gourd and potatoes and fry carefully for 2 minutes. Add a little water and simmer till required gravy is left.

Curried Plantains

6 raw plantains

Grind to a paste
6 cloves garlic
2 onions
2 red chillies
2 tbsp coriander seeds
$\frac{1}{2}$ tsp cumin seeds
$\frac{1}{2}$ tsp aniseeds

salt to taste
$\frac{1}{2}$ cup curd
$\frac{1}{2}$ tsp garam masala
a pinch salt
1 cup water
ghee for cooking and frying

Peel bananas and split them lengthwise. Scoop out a little from the centre of both halves lengthwise to fill in the masala.

Heat 1 tbsp ghee, fry the masala till golden brown, add ¼ cup curd and garam masala and cook till semi-dry. Cool and fill in plantains and secure the two halves of each with toothpicks or tie with thread. Heat ghee and fry plantains till brown. Beat the remaining curd and salt, pour on fried bananas and cook for a while. Add ½ cup hot water if necessary and cook till dry. Garnish with chopped coriander.

Baghara Baingan

$^1/_2$ kg long variety brinjals
oil for frying

Grind to a paste
1 tbsp roasted coriander seeds
4 red chillies
6 flakes garlic fried in a little oil
2 onions
2 tbsp coconut gratings

Soak and squeeze out juice
1 lemon size ball tamarind
$1^1/_2$ cups water

1 tbsp jaggery
1 tsp turmeric powder
salt to taste

Tarka
$^1/_4$ tsp mustard seeds
1 sprig curry leaves
1 tsp oil

Slit brinjals lengthwise in quarters without separating the pieces. Apply a little turmeric and salt and deep fry till golden brown. Drain and keep aside. Boil tamarind juice, ground paste, turmeric, salt and jaggery together for 5 minutes. Add fried brinjals carefully and cook till gravy thickens. Put in a serving dish. Heat 1 tsp oil, splutter mustard seeds and curry leaves and add to the brinjal curry.

Brinjal-Tomato Bharta

1 kg big, round brinjals
$^1/_4$ kg red tomatoes chopped
$^1/_2$ kg onions sliced
1 tbsp ginger cut in long, thin strips
6 green chillies
1 tbsp coriander leaves chopped
4 tbsp ghee
salt to taste

Roast brinjals on hot ashes or in hot oven. Remove skin and mash well. Heat ghee, fry onions till they change colour, add ginger strips and slit chillies and fry a little more. Add mashed brinjals and keep frying till the pulp turns golden in colour. Add chopped tomatoes and salt and fry again till ghee separates. Garnish with green coriander leaves and serve steaming hot with parathas.

Kumra
(Bihari)

1 kg red pumpkin—peel and cut in 3 cm cubes
4 tbsp ghee
1 bay leaf
1 tsp cumin seeds
1 tsp fenugreek seeds
$\frac{1}{4}$ tsp asafoetida
2 cm piece ginger ground
2 tsp salt
4 tsp coriander powder
1 tsp turmeric powder
2 red chillies
2 green chillies
$1\frac{1}{2}$ tbsp tamarind pulp
1 tsp garam masala

Heat ghee, add bay leaf, cumin seeds, fenugreek seeds, powdered asafoetida in this order and fry. Add ginger paste and pumpkin cubes. Add turmeric powder, broken red chillies and salt and fry again. Add coriander powder, cover and cook and when half done add sugar and tamarind. Cover and simmer again on slow fire till done. Sprinkle garam masala and serve.

Note: No water is needed in this cooking.

Cottage Cheese Bhaji

1 kg curd—tie in a bag and let drip overnight

Slice fine
$\frac{1}{2}$ kg onions
2 cm piece ginger
4 green chillies

2 tsp coriander powder
$\frac{1}{2}$ tsp chilli powder
$\frac{1}{4}$ tsp cinnamon powder
salt to taste
25 almonds blanched
$\frac{1}{2}$ cup peas shelled and boiled in salt water
2 tbsp ghee
1 tsp peppercorns (optional)

Heat ghee, fry ginger and chillies till brown, add onions and fry very little (do not let the onion brown). Add peppercorns and cottage cheese and other spices. Keep frying on slow fire till curd is almost dry. Add almonds and boiled peas and fry another 2-3 minutes and serve hot.

5/6/2005 – not successful

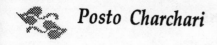

Posto Charchari

½ kg potatoes cut in 1 cm cubes
3 tbsp ghee
8 heaped tbsp poppy seeds — grind fine
2 whole red chillies broken into pieces
1½ tsp turmeric powder
1 tsp chilli powder
salt to taste
2 cups water

Heat ghee, fry potato cubes golden, drain and keep aside. In the same ghee fry broken chillies and ground paste of poppy seeds till golden brown. Add turmeric and chilli powders, salt and fry a little more. Add potato cubes and 2 cups water and cook till potatoes are soft and water well absorbed. Serve with poori, parathas or rice.

Stuffed Capsicums

4 evenly shaped good size capsicums
30 gms peas shelled and boiled
3 potatoes boiled and cubed
2 dsp onions finely chopped
1 tsp ginger chopped
1 tbsp mango or pomegranate seed powder
$1/_2$ tsp chilli powder
$1/_2$ tsp cumin seeds
$1/_4$ tsp garam masala
salt to taste
3 tbsp ghee

Put a pan of water to boil. Cut off the stem ends of capsicums and remove centres and seeds. Immerse and boil for 5 minutes in boiling water.

Heat ghee, fry chopped onions and ginger, add cumin seeds and chilli powder and then the boiled potatoes and shelled peas. Fry a little till they are well coated with ghee. Sprinkle garam masala, mango powder and salt and mash them with the ladle. Take them off the fire and cool. Pack the peppers with this mixture and replace the lids. Heat ghee in a roasting tin and when it is hot, put in the peppers and baste them well. Put them in the oven and bake for 30-35 minutes basting them with the ghee from the roasting tin, twice. Cook till tender.

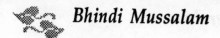# *Bhindi Mussalam*

$^1/_2$ kg tender lady's fingers

Grind to a fine paste
2 onions
2 cm piece ginger
2 flakes garlic
1 tbsp roasted coriander seed powder
$^1/_4$ tsp garam masala
1 tbsp tamarind pulp

salt and chilli powder to taste
2 tbsp ghee
$^1/_2$ cup water

Wash and wipe each lady's finger. Cut off tops and slit lengthwise taking care not to separate the two portions. Stuff the lady's fingers with the ground paste and lay them neatly on a pie-dish. Sprinkle a little salt and pour melted ghee and bake in the oven till tender.

Vegetable Casserole

250 gms French beans chopped
150 gms carrots chopped
1 cup peas shelled
12 small Patna onions peeled
3 tbsp tomato puree
1 small cauliflower broken into flowerets
1 tbsp ghee or margarine
salt and chilli powder to taste
$1^1/_2$ tbsp flour
2 eggs
$^1/_2$ cup bread crumbs
a little butter or margarine

Heat ghee, fry whole onions a little, drain and keep aside. Add 1½ level tbsp flour, brown. Add 2 cups water, salt, chilli powder, tomato puree and mix well to avoid forming lumps. Add beans, carrots, fried onions and cook for 10 minutes. Add peas and cauliflower and boil for another 5 minutes.

Take off the fire and while still hot add beaten eggs. Mix. Put in a greased casserole. Sprinkle bread crumbs, dot with a little butter or margarine and bake for 20 minutes.

Vegetarian Steamed Mould

3 carrots semi-boiled and chopped
1 cup French beans semi-boiled
1 cup shelled peas semi-boiled

White sauce
2 tbsp butter
2 tbsp flour
2 cups milk
salt and pepper to taste

3 tbsp cheese grated
a pinch mustard powder
2 eggs beaten
1 cup macaroni boiled
1 small capsicum seeded and chopped fine
bread crumbs

Boil vegetables and chop fine. Make white sauce. Take off the fire, add grated cheese, mustard powder, the beaten eggs, macaroni, capsicums and chopped vegetables. Mix thoroughly. Grease a mould, sprinkle with bread crumbs and pour in mould and steam for 25-30 minutes or till firm. Serve with extra white sauce adding a little grated cheese to it if preferred.

Egg-Vegetable Stuffed Cauliflower

1 medium cauliflower

Mix
3 hardboiled eggs chopped
2 tbsp tomato sauce
$\frac{1}{4}$ cup peas boiled
$\frac{1}{4}$ cup potatoes boiled and diced

salt to taste
1 tbsp cheese grated
2 cm square butter

Cook the cauliflower whole with a little salt till soft. Scoop out centre and pile the centre with mixture. Sprinkle with grated cheese. Put blobs of butter on top of cheese and bake in oven till brown on top.

Variation : Left-over mince meat or fish flakes with white sauce or chopped prawns can be used in place of boiled eggs.

Mince Stuffed Cauliflower

1 medium size cauliflower

Mix
100 gms mince meat
1 onion chopped
2 flakes garlic chopped
1 cm piece ginger ground
1 tsp coriander powder

2 tbsp ghee
salt and chilli powder to taste
$^1/_4$ tsp garam masala
1 onion sliced fine
1 cup tomato juice
1 tsp sugar
salt to taste

Wash cauliflower, shake off water, remove leaves, cut off stem to about 2 cms below the cauliflower.

Heat 1 tbsp ghee, add mince mixture, a cup of water and cook on slow fire till mince is tender and dry. Add salt, chilli powder and garam masala and cool.

Heat 1 tbsp ghee, fry sliced onion brown, add sugar, salt and tomato juice and cook till it becomes a thick puree.

Stuff the mince carefully in between the flowerets. Take a baking dish, grease it, put the stuffed cauliflower with stem upwards and pour the puree on it so as to cover the whole of the cauliflower. Pour half a cup of water and bake for half an hour.

Variation: The stuffed cauliflower can be cooked in a pan with a little ghee and water poured on top to soften it.

RICE

Lemon Rice

juice of 1 lime
$^1/_2$ tsp mustard seeds
1 tbsp black gram dal
16 cashewnuts
2 tbsp gingelly oil
4 green chillies split in halves
a few curry leaves
salt to taste
$^1/_8$ tsp turmeric powder
2 cups rice boiled, cooled

Heat oil in a frying pan. Splutter mustard seeds, add black gram dal and cashewnuts and fry till golden brown. Add chillies and curry leaves, fry for a second and add lemon juice, salt and turmeric. Add to cooked rice, mix well and serve.

Tamarind Rice

2 cups rice boiled, cooled
1 lemon size ball tamarind, soaked in 1 cup water
1$^1/_2$ tsp salt

Broil and powder
$^1/_4$ tsp fenugreek seeds
1 tsp black gram (urad dal)
1 pinch asafoetida

1 tsp turmeric powder
1 tbsp Bengal gram dal
1 tsp mustard seeds
6 split chillies
curry leaves
5 tbsp gingelly oil
2 tbsp peanuts shelled

Heat oil well, add mustard, Bengal gram dal, split chillies, shelled peanuts and fry till golden brown. Add masala powder, 1 cup of tamarind water, salt, turmeric and curry leaves and boil till oil separates from gravy. Mix with cooked rice and serve.

Methi Rice

Broil each separately and powder
1 tbsp Bengal gram dal
1 tbsp black gram dal
5 tbsp coriander seeds
2 cm stick cinnamon
6 dry red chillies

2 cups rice boiled, cooled
1 bunch fenugreek leaves
$^1/_2$ tsp turmeric powder
2 tbsp ghee
salt to taste

Garnish
1 tbsp butter or pure ghee
$^1/_2$ tsp mustard seeds
1 tsp black gram dal
2 tsp Bengal gram dal
a few curry leaves
juice of 1 lime
1 tbsp grated coconut

In 2 tbsp ghee add chopped fenugreek leaves, salt, turmeric and fry well on slow fire till dry. Add masala powder and rice and mix well.

Heat ghee or butter, splutter mustard seeds, add the two dals and fry for a few seconds. Take off the fire. Add curry leaves, grated coconut, and lime juice and mix with the fenugreek rice.

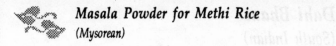

Masala Powder for Methi Rice
(Mysorean)

Fry in very little oil till brown
1 cup Bengal gram dal
1 cup black gram dal

5 cups coriander seeds
60 red chillies
7-cm piece cinnamon

Broil coriander seeds a cup at a time. Broil red chillies and cinnamon. Add to fried dals. Powder well and sieve. Bottle and keep.

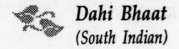

Dahi Bhaat
(South Indian)

250 gms rice boiled in salt water
1 cup milk
2 cups curd whipped
4 red chillies broken
1 tsp black gram dal
$\frac{1}{2}$ tsp mustard seeds
1 pinch asafoetida
3 cm piece ginger chopped fine
a few curry leaves
3 green chillies chopped
1 tbsp gingelly oil
salt to taste

Heat oil. Splutter red chillies, black gram, mustard seeds, asafoetida and add chopped green chillies, ginger and curry leaves. Take off the fire and mix in curd. Add this and the milk to the cooked rice and keep a few hours before serving to get a better taste.

Garnish with chopped, green coriander leaves.

Til Rice

500 gms rice—boil, drain and cool
1 tbsp ghee
20 cashewnuts—fry golden brown
1 sprig curry leaves—fry and drain

Fry in 1 tsp oil and powder
240 gms sesame seeds
4 red chillies
1 tsp black gram dal
1 pinch asafoetida

$^1/_2$ tsp mustard seeds
1 tsp black gram dal
4 green chillies chopped
2 tbsp Bengal gram dal soaked in water
salt to taste

Heat ghee. Splutter mustard seeds, black gram and chopped green chillies. Add drained Bengal gram dal and salt and fry for one minute. Add masala powder, curry leaves, cashewnuts and boiled rice. Mix well, heat and serve hot or cold as desired.

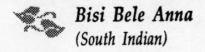

Bisi Bele Anna
(South Indian)

1 cup arhar dal (yellow lentils)
$^1/_2$ cup ghee
$^1/_2$ tsp turmeric powder
$^3/_4$ cup rice

Roast and powder
1 tsp urad dal
1 tsp chana dal
3 tsp coriander seeds
3 2-cm cinnamon sticks
4 red chillies
6 grains fenugreek seeds
a pinch asafoetida
salt to taste

3 tsp tamarind juice
1 tbsp grated coconut
2 tbsp ghee
curry leaves
10 cashewnuts
$^1/_2$ tsp mustard seeds

Cook yellow lentil dal with 1 tsp ghee and turmeric in 3 cups water. When half cooked, add washed rice and let cook till ¾ done. Add a tbsp ghee while cooking. When nearly ready add salt, powder masala, tamarind juice and coconut. Add a little water if needed and go on adding ghee every 5 minutes till you have consumed all the ghee. Cook for another five minutes.

Heat 2 tbsp ghee in a pan, add mustard seeds and brown cashewnuts. Take off the fire, add curry leaves and pour this over cooked rice. Mix well and serve hot.

Note: Vegetables like brinjals, onions and potatoes can be added when the rice is cooked 90%.

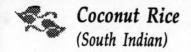

Coconut Rice
(South Indian)

3 cups Basmati or Patna rice
3 tbsp ghee
3 onions sliced
10 cardamoms
5 cm stick cinnamon
1 coconut—extract 1 ltr milk by adding water
20 cashewnuts
1 tsp salt

Lightly fry the onions in ghee. Add cardamoms, cinnamon and cashewnuts and fry a while. Add drained rice and fry for two minutes. Add coconut-milk and salt and cook on strong fire. As soon as holes appear on top layer of rice, reduce flame and cook on very low heat till water is absorbed and the grains become soft and dry.

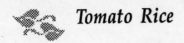

Tomato Rice

500 gms rice—wash and soak for $\frac{1}{2}$ an hr
$\frac{1}{2}$ kg tomatoes—boil in water and strain 5 cups juice
2 onions thinly sliced
2 cm piece ginger thinly sliced
1 tsp cumin seeds
2 bay leaves
2 tbsp ghee
salt to taste
3 potatoes—cut in fingers and fry
2 onions—slice and brown

Heat ghee, half brown onions, add ginger and fry till onions are golden brown. Add cumin seeds, bay leaf and fry for one minute. Add strained rice and fry till rice is well coated with ghee. Pour the tomato juice and salt, adding a little water if needed to cook the rice well. Garnish with browned onions and fried potato fingers.

Delicious Vegetable Biryani

250 gms Patna rice—clean and soak for ¹/₂ an hr
100 gms masur dal—clean and soak for ¹/₂ an hr
4 tbsp ghee
6 cloves
5 cm stick cinnamon
1 coconut—grind and extract 2 cups juice
4 tomatoes—make puree
4 tbsp curd beaten
salt to taste
40 raisins
20 almonds or cashewnuts sliced

Boil till tender
4 potatoes—slice and fry golden brown
4 carrots—dice and fry for 3 mins
1 cup peas—shell and fry for 3 mins
1 cup water

Grind to a paste
1 tsp cumin seeds
4 red chillies
2 onions
1 tsp turmeric powder

In a pan, heat ghee, fry cloves, cinnamon and ground paste till brown. Add drained rice and dal and stir-fry for another 5 minutes. Add 2 cups coconut juice, tomato puree and and the left-over gravy from the boiled vegetables. When half cooked, add vegetables, salt and curd and cook again on very slow fire till dry. Garnish with raisins and almonds and serve steaming hot with knobs of butter served on each helping.

Vegetable Pulao

Boil each separately in salt water and drain
2 carrots cut in cubes
1 cup shelled peas
$^1/_2$ cup sliced French beans
1 small cauliflower cut in small pieces

Boil till nearly tender, drain and cool
500 gms good quality rice
$^1/_4$ tsp turmeric powder
salt to taste
6 cups water

3 tbsp ghee
2 level tsp sugar
3 onions sliced thin
2 cm stick cinnamon broken in bits
8 cardamoms
6 cloves
1 tsp cumin seeds
20 raisins
10 cashewnuts

Heat ghee, brown sugar and onions, splutter garam masala, add the raisins and cashewnuts and fry for 2 minutes. Add boiled vegetables and fry for one minute. Finally add the boiled rice. Mix carefully and bake in covered pan for 10-15 minutes. Serve hot.

To check if the rice is boiled properly — take a grain of rice and press it between the thumb and the first finger tip. If you find one or two white granules still uncooked, the rice is ready to be drained and cooled.

Tahiri
(U.P.)

2½ cups Basmati or Patna rice
1 kg green peas shelled
2 onions sliced
1 bay leaf
10 cardamoms
2 cm stick cinnamon
6 cloves
10 peppercorns
1 tsp cumin seeds
1 tsp garam masala
1 tsp chilli powder
2 tsp salt
1 ltr water
oil for frying

Clean and soak rice in water for 20-30 minutes. Heat 1½ tbsp oil, fry chopped onions brown. Add cardamoms, cinnamon, cloves, bay leaf, peppercorns and cumin seeds and when they stop spluttering, add washed peas and cover pan with lid for five minutes. Take lid off and add chilli powder and garam masala and fry for a while. Add drained rice and fry again for 3 minutes or till rice is also fried slightly. Add salt and pour water over it. Mix well and cover. Increase the fire and let boil till you see holes on the top layer. Take off the fire and put in moderate oven for 15 minutes. Serve hot with cubes of butter put in each individual helping.

Note : If oven is not available, reduce heat to minimum and cook for 15 minutes stirring with the back of a spoon occasionally so that the rice does not stick or get burnt at the bottom.

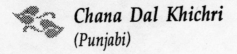

Chana Dal Khichri
(Punjabi)

1 cup Bengal gram dal
1 cup Basmati rice—soak for $\frac{1}{2}$ an hr
2 tbsp pure ghee
1 tsp cumin seeds
5 cm stick cinnamon broken
10 cardamoms split open
1 bay leaf
8 peppercorns
salt to taste

Boil Bengal gram dal in 3 cups water till nearly done. Drain and keep liquid aside. Heat ghee and fry masalas. Add drained rice and fry for 1 minute. Add water to liquid in which Bengal gram dal was boiled to make 2½ cups. Add this water to fried rice and give one quick boil. Add boiled dal, cover and let cook on strong fire till holes appear on top of rice. Take off the fire and put in a slow oven for 15-20 minutes.

Serve hot with home-made butter.

Khichuri
(Bengali)

1 cup rice
$^1/_2$ cup moong dal—broil
$^1/_2$ cup masur dal

2 tbsp ghee
1 bay leaf
8 cardamoms
6 cloves
5 cm stick cinnamon
2 onions—slice fine
1 tsp turmeric powder
salt to taste
1 tbsp sugar
3 potatoes cut in halves
1 cup peas shelled
1 small cauliflower cut in flowerets
6 green chillies ground

Grind fine
$2^1/_2$ tsp coriander seeds
2 cm piece ginger
$1^1/_2$ tsp cumin seeds

In ghee add whole garam masalas and sliced onions and fry till golden in colour. Add drained rice and dals and fry till rice is also fried a bit. Add turmeric powder and ground paste and fry again for 2 minutes. Add 5 cups water with 1 tbsp sugar and salt to taste. When half done, add potatoes, peas, cauliflower and ground chillies. Simmer on slow fire till vegetables are tender.

Zafrani Pulao

1 cup rice—half boil, drain and cool
2 tbsp ghee
3 tbsp sugar
10 almonds blanched
30 raisins—clean and lightly fry
1 tbsp dry coconut—cut in $^1/_2$ cm cubes and lightly fry
6 cardamoms—shell and crush coarsely
1 tsp saffron soaked in 3 tbsp hot milk

Divide rice in three parts. Heat 1 tbsp ghee, put first part rice and top with half the sugar, coconut, almonds, raisins and cardamom powder. Repeat this and spread third part rice. Pour saffron milk all over this top layer. Heat 1 tbsp ghee and pour on top. Put lid on pan and keep on hot ashes with a few live coals on top for 10-15 minutes till rice is done and the grains are dry or put in a moderate oven for 10 minutes or more till dry.

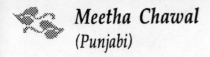

Meetha Chawal
(Punjabi)

250 gms Basmati rice—half boil with
   a pinch of salt and drain

Boil on slow fire till sugar is dissolved
3 cups water
250 gms sugar
$\frac{1}{2}$ tsp saffron

4 tbsp pure ghee
seeds of 6 green cardamoms
6 cloves
25 raisins
20 almonds—blanch and cut in halves
1 silver leaf

Heat ghee, add cardamom seeds and cloves and splutter. Add raisins and fry, adding the boiled rice. Fry till rice is well coated with ghee. Pour sugar syrup and cook on brisk fire for five minutes. Reduce heat and simmer till rice is done and liquid dries up. Serve this rice garnished with the blanched almonds rolled in silver leaf.

Mutton Biryani

1 cup Patna rice—add salt and half boil
250 gms mutton cut in pieces
3 onions—slice, brown and crush

Grind to a paste
2 onions
1 pod garlic
2 cm piece ginger
1 tbsp coriander leaves
6 green chillies
2 tsp poppy seeds
2 cm stick cinnamon
1 blade mace
1 bay leaf
6 cloves
8 cardamoms
2 tsp scraped coconut
salt to taste

2 cups curd
$^1/_2$ tsp saffron soaked in 2 tsp milk
4 tbsp ghee
12 almonds
12 cashewnuts
20 raisins
3 eggs hard-boiled

Beat curd, add masala paste, mutton pieces, fried, crushed onions and salt and marinate for 4 hours. Cook over low heat till mutton is done and a little gravy remains.

In a thick bottomed pan put 1 tbsp ghee and a third of the rice, then a layer of mutton with a little gravy, a layer of rice, a layer of mutton and gravy and lastly a layer of rice. Dot generously with ghee and sprinkle soaked saffron. Cover with lid and bake in a moderate oven for 15 minutes.

Garnish with fried nuts and eggs.

Yakhni Pulao

$^{1}/_{2}$ kg mutton
salt to taste
4 cups water
1 cup Patna rice—wash and soak for 15 mins
2 onions sliced
1 cup curd
1 tsp cumin seeds
2 cm stick cinnamon
3 cloves
6 cardamoms
$^{1}/_{2}$ tsp garlic paste
$^{1}/_{2}$ tsp ginger paste
salt to taste
4 tbsp ghee

Make a bouquet garni
1 onion chopped
10 cloves garlic
2 cm piece ginger chopped
2 cm stick cinnamon
6 cloves
1 tbsp coriander seeds

For garnish
4 large onions thinly sliced, crisp-fried
4 hard-boiled eggs, shelled, sliced

Boil mutton, salt, bouquet garni, in 4 cups water on slow fire till mutton is tender. Squeeze the bouquet garni and discard it (keep 2 cups gravy — Yakhni).

Heat ghee in a thick bottomed pan and fry sliced onions brown. Add all the masalas and fry till the raw smell of garlic and ginger disappears. Add mutton pieces, salt and curd and fry till mutton is brown. Add rice and fry again till rice is golden brown. Add Yakhni and cook till rice is nearly done and water evaporates. Put in oven for 10 minutes and bake. Serve hot garnished with browned onions and boiled eggs.

Mutanjan
(Kashmiri)

$^1/_2$ kg mutton
salt
1 tbsp lemon juice
1 tbsp sugar
250 gms Basmati rice
30 pine nuts or almonds
3 tbsp ghee or oil

4 cloves
8 peppercorns
4 cardamoms
1 bay leaf
2 cm stick cinnamon

Make a bouquet garni
5 cm stick cinnamon
6 cloves
10 peppercorns
2 tsp coriander seeds
8 cardamoms
2 onions chopped

Soak
$^1/_2$ tsp saffron
2 tsp milk

In a pan, boil mutton with 4 cups water, ½ tsp salt and bouquet garni till 2 cups gravy remains. Remove bouquet garni, squeeze out juice well and cook till 1 cup liquid remains. Add sugar and lemon juice and cook 2 minutes.

In another pan boil the rice with the second lot of ingredients and a little salt and cook till a grain of rice pressed between the thumb and forefinger leaves two white uncooked granules. Drain, remove bay leaf and cool.

In a heavy bottomed pan put 1 tbsp ghee and sandwich the mutton and gravy between 2 layers of rice. Sprinkle with saffron and dot generously with 2 tbsp ghee. Cover and bake in a moderate oven till rice is tender and gravy is absorbed.

Garnish with fried nuts.

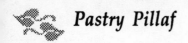

Pastry Pillaf

6 tbsp margarine
8 heaped tbsp flour
2 egg yolks or milk
salt and pepper to taste

For the filling
Use Kashmiri Mutanjan

Rub margarine into the flour, until it has the consistency of bread crumbs. Add seasoning. Make into firm dough with egg yolks or milk. Roll into a ball, then wrap in waxed paper and keep in the refrigerator for one hour. Divide dough in two parts (2 : 1). Roll out first portion to 35 cm diameter and line the base and sides of a 20 cm cake tin with it. Put alternate layers of rice and cooked mutton, finishing with a layer of rice. Sprinkle with saffron in milk and nuts. Roll the second part of dough to cover the top of the cake tin and put a little melted fat all over and around the pastry and bake till pastry is golden brown.

Invert and serve.

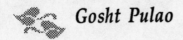

Gosht Pulao

Boil on slow fire till meat is tender
1 kg mutton
6 cups water
5 cm stick cinnamon
2 bay leaves
2 tsp salt

600 gms Basmati rice—wash and
  soak for $^1/_2$ an hr and strain
5 tbsp ghee
3 onions sliced
10 cardamoms
5 cloves
15 peppercorns
1 tsp salt

Strain meat and keep yakhni for cooking the rice in, discarding the bay leaves and cinnamon stick.

Heat ghee, fry boiled pieces of mutton till brown. Remove. In the same ghee fry sliced onions till golden brown. Add cardamoms, cloves, peppercorns and the strained rice and fry till rice changes colour. Add mutton pieces, salt and the yakhni in which mutton was boiled, adding more water to make it upto 6 cups. Cook on brisk fire till holes appear on top layer of rice. Bake in moderate oven and serve hot.

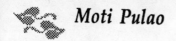

Moti Pulao

250 gms mince meat
2 tsp coriander powder
$\frac{1}{2}$ tsp garam masala
a little salt
100 gms ghee
2 onions sliced
1 pod garlic chopped
8 cardamoms
1 tsp cumin seeds
$\frac{1}{2}$ cup thick curd
salt to taste
2 cups rice boiled in salt water
2 onions sliced and fried brown

Mix and mash the first four ingredients. Shape into tiny balls and boil in 1 cup of water till balls are fully cooked. Drain and keep the liquid aside.

Heat ghee in a pan, fry onions and garlic till golden brown. Add cumin seeds and cardamoms and when they splutter add beaten curd and salt. Cook for 3 minutes and then add the meat balls and fry again. Sprinkle the remaining yakhni till the balls are well cooked and dry. Add the boiled rice and mix well. Serve garnished with fried onions.

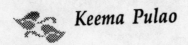

Keema Pulao

½ kg Basmati or Patna rice—soak for 15 mins
4 tbsp ghee
2 onions sliced
½ kg mince meat
1 cup curd
2 cm piece ginger sliced
1 tsp chilli powder
1 tsp garam masala
1 tbsp coriander powder
salt to taste
1 ltr milk
1 tsp saffron

Heat ghee, fry sliced onions till brown. Add mince, curd, ginger, chilli powder, garam masala, coriander powder and salt and let cook on very slow fire adding a little water till mince is tender and nicely browned. Add drained rice, 1 litre milk (in which saffron has been soaked) and cook on strong fire till holes appear on top layer of rice. Reduce heat to the lowest and cook for 15 minutes keeping a griddle under the pan to prevent rice from burning. Or bake in slow oven for 15 minutes.

Mince and Rice Casserole

3 tbsp oil
1 clove garlic crushed
3 onions chopped
750 gms mince meat
4 tomatoes chopped
1 cup stock or water
1 tsp garam masala
salt to taste
1 tsp Worcestershire sauce
1 cup grated cheese
2 tbsp butter
400 gms rice boiled in little salt water and drained

Heat oil in a large frying pan, fry the crushed garlic and chopped onions till lightly browned. Add mince and brown, stirring constantly. Add chopped tomatoes and cook till they become pulpy. Add stock or water, garam masala, sauce and salt to taste. Cook till mince is well done and dry. Add rice to the mince, mix carefully and put it in a casserole dish, topping it with grated cheese. Dot with butter and bake for 10 minutes in a moderate oven.

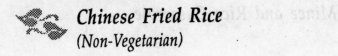

Chinese Fried Rice
(Non-Vegetarian)

2 large platefuls boiled, cooled rice
4 tbsp groundnut oil
4 onions diced
5 eggs beaten
1 cup meat or chicken shredded
3 tsp salt
$2^1/_2$ tbsp soya sauce

On high fire fry onions in oil, add rice and fry till it is slightly brown. Put in beaten eggs, turning the rice quickly so as to coat the grains of rice. Add shredded meat or chicken and fry for another five minutes. Add salt, soya sauce and serve very hot.

Chicken Pulao

1 large chicken
1 large onion chopped
6 cloves
5-cm stick cinnamon broken
1 bay leaf
2 tsp coriander seeds
4 black cardamoms crushed
2 tbsp fennel seeds
6 cups water
salt to taste
3 tbsp ghee
1 tsp cumin seeds
1 tsp turmeric powder
500 gms Basmati rice
3 large onions finely sliced, crisp fried

Wash and soak rice for ½ an hour.

In a large pan with a lid combine the first nine ingredients and boil till the chicken is 80% tender. Take out the whole chicken and remove flesh. Put the bones back into the pan and boil again for another ½ an hour. Take off the fire, drain liquid and keep aside.

In a flat bottomed pan heat ghee, splutter cumin seeds. Add turmeric powder and chicken pieces and fry till golden brown. Add drained rice, salt and drained masala liquid to come upto 3 cms above the surface of the rice and cook on a high flame till holes appear on the surface. Reduce heat and cook till rice is tender and the grains separate. Garnish with fried onions and serve steaming hot.

ROTIS

Ma-Poli

Knead well and form into 8 balls
$^1/_2$ cup gram flour
$^1/_2$ cup rice flour
1 cup boiling water
1 tbsp ghee
salt to taste
1 tsp chilli powder

Knead to soft dough and form into 8 balls
$^1/_2$ cup flour
$^1/_2$ cup water
$^1/_2$ tsp cardamom powder
salt to taste
1 tbsp ghee

Grease hands. Take one flour ball, flatten it and stuff with rice ball. Roll on a greased board like a chapati, bake on hot griddle for a minute each side and then pour melted ghee and fry both sides till they are golden brown.

Serve hot. Stuffing can be changed, adding sugar and coconut to rice flour, instead of gram flour, salt and chillies.

Chigri

Make soft dough with water
1 cup wheat flour
1 tbsp ghee
salt to taste
$^1/_4$ tsp carom seeds
2 tbsp ghee

Heat griddle. Make a thick chapati of dough with hand and lay on griddle for half a minute. Take it off the griddle and add 1 tbsp ghee in it. Mix well and form a handmade chapati and lay on griddle again for half a minute. Take off the fire and mix well again with hand, adding the last tbsp ghee and knead the dough well again. With the help of a rolling pin and board roll into ½ cm thick chapati and bake on griddle on very slow fire till both sides are done and golden brown in colour. Serve with butter.

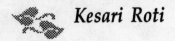

Kesari Roti

Knead to a soft dough with cold milk
500 gms flour
1 tsp salt
2 tbsp ghee

ghee for layers and frying
little flour for sprinkling between layers

Mix and keep
$1/2$ tsp saffron
$1/4$ cup milk

Roll out ten chapatis of equal size. Brush the first chapati with ghee, sprinkle flour, lay the second chapati and do the same till the ninth chapati is sprinkled with flour. Lay the tenth chapati and roll carefully the ten layers together to make one big and thick chapati. Perforate with fork all over and lay on a baking sheet. Bake in moderate oven for 8 to 10 minutes till both sides are done. Brush with milk mixture on both sides and bake again for a few minutes till you get a sheen on both sides. Serve hot.

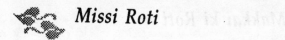

Missi Roti

1 cup wheat flour
1 cup whole gram flour
1 tsp chilli powder or
6 green chillies chopped fine
2 onions chopped fine
salt to taste
ghee for frying

Mix the two flours, the chillies, onions and salt. Add 2 tbsp melted ghee and mix well. Add some hot water and make a stiff dough. Cover and keep for 45 minutes (to allow the gram flour to swell). Knead again. Divide into 12 equal portions. Pull each portion lengthwise and flatten it. Apply a little melted fat and roll into pencil shape. Coil it into a ball, press it and roll with a rolling pin to 12 cm diameter each. Heat griddle, bake dry till both sides are done, pour a tsp fat on top surface and turn. Press it with a fish slice and keep moving and pressing, frying on slow fire. Turn and do the same to the other side till both sides are golden brown and crisp. Serve hot with curd.

Missi Makkai ki Roti

500 gms maize flour
1 cup fenugreek leaves chopped, boiled
1 tsp chilli powder
salt to taste
hot water
1 tbsp ghee for dough
ghee for frying
4 tbsp butter

Sieve maize flour in a basin. Add salt, ghee, cooked fenugreek and mix well. Separate enough flour mixture to make one roti, add enough hot water and prepare a stiff dough kneading well with the ball of your hand. Shape round thick roti between your two palms. Bake on hot griddle over slow fire on both sides. When nearly done pour a little fat and fry both sides till golden brown in colour. Take off the griddle and pinch in four or five places on one side of roti. Put butter in the depressions thus made and serve hot. Knead and bake each roti and follow the same procedure as above.

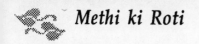

Methi ki Roti

1 cup wheat flour
50 gms fenugreek leaves chopped
25 gms coriander leaves chopped
6 green chillies chopped
salt to taste
1 tbsp ghee
2 tbsp ghee for frying

Make a stiff dough with wheat flour, cold water, 1 tbsp ghee and other ingredients. Cover and keep for half an hour. Knead again. Roll into parathas, bake both sides on griddle and when nearly done apply fat on both sides and fry till golden brown.

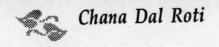

Chana Dal Roti

1 cup Bengal gram dal boiled, drained
$^1/_2$ tsp cumin seeds
$^3/_4$ tsp chilli powder
1 tbsp roasted coriander seed powder
salt to taste
1 tsp ginger very finely chopped
1 tbsp coriander leaves chopped fine
ghee for frying
250 gms wheat flour
salt to taste
enough cold water to knead dough

Heat one tbsp ghee in a frying pan. Add cumin seeds and chilli powder, then the Bengal gram dal, coriander powder, ginger, coriander leaves and the salt. Fry for 5 minutes and cool.

Make dough with wheat flour adding salt to it. Divide it into 12 portions. Also divide dal into 12 portions. Fill each portion with dal stuffing. Roll into parathas and fry like ordinary parathas.

Kulcha

$^1/_2$ kg flour
1 tsp yeast
$^1/_2$ tsp sugar
$^1/_2$ cup lukewarm water
2 eggs beaten
salt to taste
1 cup curd

Mix yeast, and sugar in lukewarm water and leave to rise for 10-15 minutes. Mix flour, salt and curd to yeast mixture and knead well, adding egg mixture. Keep in a covered pan in a warm place and let rise for two hours. Punch it down, divide dough into 6 equal parts and make round balls. Shape into round thick pooris and keep in a greased tray to rise (40 minutes). Brush with milk or beaten egg before baking in a hot oven at 200°C for 15 minutes.

Serve with kabuli chana and mint chutney.

Naan

1 kg flour
1 level tsp baking powder
1 tsp salt
30 gms ghee (melted)
1 egg (big size)
$^3/_4$ cup milk
$1^1/_4$ cups curd
1 tsp powdered sugar
1 level tsp nigella seeds
1 tbsp poppy seeds

Sieve flour, baking powder, salt and sugar. Add melted ghee and mix with tips of fingers. Beat egg, mix with milk and add to powder ingredients. Mix well, adding a few tbsp cold water. Then add the beaten curd and knead for a long time till dough is smooth and elastic. Divide into 8 balls, cover with wet cloth and keep for half an hour. Shape into naans. Moisten one side. Apply a little nigella and poppy seeds on the other side and bake in tandoor. Serve immediately.

Badshahi Naan

$^1/_2$ kg flour
$^1/_2$ tsp granulated yeast
1 tsp sugar
$^1/_4$ cup lukewarm water
$^1/_4$ cup milk scalded and cooled
salt to taste
1 egg beaten
2 tbsp butter
$^1/_2$ tsp nigella seeds
ghee for deep frying

Mix yeast, sugar and lukewarm water and let stand for 10 minutes. Sieve flour and salt, add butter and rub till mixture is crumbly. Then add yeast, warm milk and the beaten egg and knead into a smooth dough. Roll into a ball and put in a bowl. Cover with damp cloth and keep in a warm place to rise till double in bulk. Punch down and make into 8 balls and roll into 2 cm thickness. Lay on a greased tray and sprinkle nigella seeds and let them rise again till double in size. Bake in a very hot oven till done.

Bhakhri

500 gms wheat flour
1 cup sour curd
1 tsp chilli powder
1 tsp garam masala
a pinch asafoetida mixed in 1 tsp water
$^1/_2$ tsp carom seeds
2 heaped tbsp ghee
salt to taste
ghee for frying

Sieve flour and the dry ingredients. Rub in solid ghee with hands, add beaten curd and asafoetida, water and carom seeds. Use a little water and knead into smooth dough. Cover and keep for an hour. Roll into 10 chapatis. Perforate each with fork and fry like parathas.

Bati
(Rajasthani)

Make hard dough as for pooris
250 gms wheat flour
1 cup curd
salt to taste
1 tbsp ghee
ghee for frying

Boil 4 cups water with a tsp salt. Make 20 even size balls with dough. Press in the palms of both hands and press in the centre with thumb and boil them for 15 minutes. Drain water and slit each one crosswise taking care not to cut right down. Deep fry each one golden brown and serve with pure melted ghee on top of each.

Kutlame

Make into dough and keep for ¹/₂ an hr
500 gms flour
1 tsp salt
1 tbsp ghee
1¹/₄ cups warm water

Beat to a creamy mixture
2 tbsp rice flour
1 tbsp ghee

ghee for frying

Roll dough in a thick round, spread creamy mixture evenly and roll up. Fold it vertically and roll again. Cut into 7 cm pooris with a sharp lid. Deep fry until light brown and well risen.

Dogri Bhatura

¹/₂ kg flour
¹/₂ tsp soda-bi-carb
2 tbsp melted ghee
salt to taste
1 cup curd
ghee for frying

Sieve soda, salt and flour. Add ghee and mix well. Knead with curd till smooth. In a greased pan put this dough and cover with wet cloth. Keep in a warm place till it is double in bulk (8-10 hours). Divide in 12 equal size portions, roll lightly on board into 10-cm rounds and deep fry.

Yeast Bhatura

¹/₂ kg flour
1 level tsp dry yeast
1 level tsp sugar
³/₄ cup lukewarm water
salt to taste
1 cup curd
ghee for frying

Mix yeast, sugar and lukewarm water. Cover and keep for 10 minutes to rise. Make a dough with flour, curd, salt and yeast. Knead well, cover and keep aside in a warm place to rise. When double in bulk, divide dough in small portions (walnut size). Roll out ¼ cm thin and half fry in hot ghee. Do not brown, but remove as soon as each side swells a little. Drain and keep aside. Before serving, cook each one on a griddle, pressing down with fish slice so as to brown and make crisp.

Yeast begins to activate at about 10°C and is at its best between 23°C to 28°C. It begins to die around 49°C and is useless for baking after 62°C.

Khasta Kachowri

1 cup black gram dal—soak in water overnight
ghee for frying dal paste

Grind along with dal
1 tsp cumin seeds
$^1/_2$ tsp chilli powder
salt to taste
$1^1/_2$ tsp coriander powder
a pinch asafoetida

Make a hard dough with a little water
and leave for 1 hr
2 cups flour
2 tbsp ghee
1 tsp salt
pinch soda-bi-carb

Heat 1 tbsp ghee, add dal paste and fry well till golden brown. Do not add water. Cool.

Divide dough into 16 rounds; shape into cups with the tips of the finger. Place in the hollow a tbsp fried dal. Close up the cup and press between the palms of both hands into round and slightly pressed cakes.

Deep fry in ghee on slow fire, till they puff up and become crisp and golden.

Thoda
(Punjabi)

250 gms maize flour
150 gms jaggery
2 tbsp ghee
1 cup water
ghee for frying

Make thick syrup of jaggery with a cup of water. Heat ghee, add to flour and knead with jaggery syrup. Heat griddle and apply a little ghee all over. Divide dough in 5 equal balls. Knead one ball at a time with the ball of your hand. Shape into thick roti and bake on griddle till both sides are done. Pour melted ghee and fry on very slow fire till both sides turn golden brown. Make the other four like this.

Can be kept for 3-4 days.

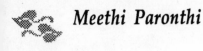

Meethi Paronthi

250 gms wheat flour
$^1/_4$ tsp salt
4 heaped tbsp ghee
12 tbsp sugar

Make soft dough with wheat flour and salt and keep for one hour. Knead again before making parathas.

Divide dough into 8 balls. Flatten each ball with hand, apply a little ghee and shape into a cup. Place 1½ tbsp sugar in the hollow of each. Close up and press between the palms of both hands and roll out into 12 cm circles, taking care not to allow sugar to come out. Bake both sides on hot griddle. Pour 1 tbsp ghee and fry like parathas on very slow fire allowing the sugar inside to melt and become syrupy. Remove from griddle carefully and serve hot.

If you do not find it easy, divide dough into 16 balls and roll out 16 chapatis. Lay one, spread with a little ghee, spread 1½ tbsp sugar, cover with second chapati, press sides and roll a little more and fry as for parathas.

Potato Paratha

$^{1}/_{2}$ cup wheat flour
$^{1}/_{2}$ cup flour
1 tsp salt
1 tbsp ghee

Mix and mash
$1^{1}/_{2}$ cups boiled and mashed potatoes
$^{1}/_{2}$ tsp garam masala
$^{3}/_{4}$ tsp chilli powder
1 tbsp roasted coriander seed powder
1 tbsp chopped coriander leaves
2 tbsp onions chopped fine
salt to taste

Mix wheat flour, flour and salt. Rub in the ghee with the tips of your fingers. Add cold water and make a soft dough. Knead well. Divide dough into ten portions. Also divide filling in 10 equal portions. Roll each dough into a small poori, place stuffing in centre, cover and roll in the palms of your hand to make a round ball. Using a rolling pin and dry flour, roll into 20 cm size circles taking care that the filling does not come out. Heat a griddle and fry just like plain parathas till they are brown and crisp. Serve hot.

Note: 1 tsp pomegranate seed powder can be added to the filling.

Savoury Paratha

1 cup gram flour
1 cup flour
1 heaped tbsp ghee
1 heaped tbsp coriander leaves chopped
4 green chillies chopped fine
1 tsp carom seeds
salt to taste
cold water to make dough
ghee for frying

Mix all the ingredients, add water and make a stiff dough. Cover and keep for half an hour. Roll into parathas and fry on very slow fire on a griddle. Serve very hot. They are very crisp. Makes 12.

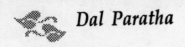

Dal Paratha

1 cup black gram dal—soak for 2 hrs and grind fine

Grind to a paste
1 tbsp cumin seeds
2 cardamoms
2 cm stick cinnamon
6 red chillies

salt to taste
1 pinch asafoetida
ghee for frying gram paste
1½ cups flour or whole wheat flour
salt to taste
1 tbsp ghee

Rub ghee in flour, add salt, knead to a soft dough and keep aside. Heat ghee, add asafoetida, the masala paste and the dal paste and fry till moisture is absorbed and raw smell disappears. Cool.

Divide dough in 8 balls. Stuff each one with cooled dal paste. Roll thin like a chapati and fry like a paratha.

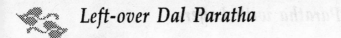

Left-over Dal Paratha

1 cup cooked dal (any left-over dal)
1¹/₂ cups wheat flour
1 onion chopped very fine
2 tsp roasted coriander seed powder
¹/₂ tsp chilli powder
¹/₄ tsp carom seeds
1 tbsp melted ghee
ghee for frying

In a basin put left-over dal, sieve the wheat flour over it. Add all the other ingredients and knead well. Use water only if necessary. Divide dough into 5 parts. Pull each piece sideways, apply a tsp ghee in each, fold and roll into a long shape. Coil into a ball and roll it into a flat chapati. Bake it on a dry griddle and when both sides are done, put 2 tsp ghee and fry both sides, pressing and rubbing it with a flat spoon while frying, to make it more crisp. Serve each with a knob of butter. Can be eaten cold also.

Note : If the dal is too runny, cook and thicken it to make it semi-solid before adding wheat flour.

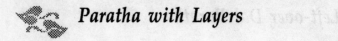

Paratha with Layers

3 cups flour or whole wheat flour
1 tsp salt
2 tbsp ghee
water to knead
6 tbsp ghee for frying

Rub 2 tbsp ghee in flour, add salt and knead well with lukewarm water. Divide dough into 16 balls. Roll each ball like a chapati, smear ghee and sprinkle a little dry flour. Take a sharp knife and from the centre cut up to the edge. Roll from one side, shaping like a horn. Open the edge portion of horn, shape and press horn flat and roll in a chapati shape again. Bake on hot griddle over slow fire and when both sides are half-done pour little melted ghee around edges and fry both sides crisp.

Serve hot.

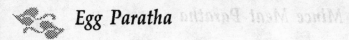

Egg Paratha

Knead to a very soft dough with hot water
250 gms flour
salt to taste
1 tbsp ghee

Chop very fine
1 onion
1 tbsp coriander leaves
2 green chillies

2 eggs beaten well
salt to taste
ghee for frying

Mix eggs with chopped stuff, add salt. Divide dough into 9 balls. Roll each ball thin, one at a time, and spread 1 tbsp egg batter on each. Fold from four sides, pat again with greased hands and fry on hot griddle like parathas. Serve piping hot.

Mince Meat Paratha

¹/₂ kg mince meat
2 onions
1 pod garlic
2 green chillies
1 cm piece ginger
1 tbsp coriander leaves
1 tsp garam masala
1 tbsp coriander powder
2 tomatoes
salt to taste
2 tbsp ghee
ghee for frying parathas

Knead with warm water to soft dough
and keep for 1 hr
250 gms flour
1 tsp salt
1 tbsp ghee

Chop onions, garlic, chillies, ginger, coriander leaves and tomatoes.

Heat ghee. Fry onions and garlic till light brown. Add chillies, ginger, mince meat, tomatoes, salt and all the other masalas. Add ½ cup water and cook till dry and meat is done and ghee separates.

Divide dough into 8 balls and proceed as for Meethi Paronthi.

PICKLES

Hot Mango Pickle

2 kg mangoes—peel and slice in finger size pieces
2 cups salt
2 tsp turmeric powder
200 gms red chilli powder
3 tbsp turmeric powder
4 tbsp mustard seed powder
1 tsp fenugreek seeds roasted and powdered
3 cups gingelly oil
1$\frac{1}{2}$ cups vinegar
1 tsp fenugreek seeds
2 tsp cumin seeds
2 tsp mustard seeds

Apply 1 cup salt and 2 tsp turmeric to sliced mangoes and sun them for 2 days. On 3rd day remove from salt-water and dry them in the sun. Retain salt water.

Heat oil, splutter mustard, fenugreek and cumin seeds. Add turmeric, chilli, mustard and fenugreek powders. Add salt water and vinegar and cook for 5 minutes adding additional salt. Remove from fire, cool and add dried mango pieces. Mix well and fill in jars.

Whole Mango Pickle

1½ kg small green mangoes
3 tbsp salt
1 tbsp garlic chopped
1½ tbsp ginger chopped
4 tbsp chilli powder
6 tbsp mustard seeds roasted and husked

Broil and powder
6 tbsp cumin seeds
3 tbsp fenugreek seeds
1 tbsp black cumin seeds

2 tbsp turmeric powder
salt to taste for masala only
1 kg mustard oil
1 tbsp nigella seeds

Wash, wipe and slit mango tops. Cut into quarters half-way down only. Remove kernels, rub and fill with salt. Place in a basket and dry in sun for 3-4 days.

Heat one cup oil, fry garlic and ginger, add nigella seeds and splutter. Add all the powders and the husked mustard seeds, fry well and add salt to taste (for the masala). Fill each mango with masala, lay in a jar carefully and pour the rest of the oil to cover mangoes. Keep in the sun for a week to 10 days. Keep in a dry dark place.

Note: If more pungency is wanted, boil a bottle of vinegar with oil and pour over mangoes before preserving.

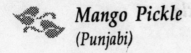

Mango Pickle
(Punjabi)

2 kg tart, green mangoes
250 gms rock salt
100 gms chilli powder
50 gms aniseeds
30 gms fenugreek seeds
30 gms nigella seeds
1 kg mustard oil
3 tbsp turmeric powder
pea size piece asafoetida

Wash, wipe and cut mangoes into 8 parts each, remove kernels, apply half the salt and let drain for 5-6 hours in the sun. (Do this in the morning so that the mangoes are ready by evening). Heat mustard oil till smoking hot and fry a pinch of asafoetida in it and mash it well. Cool oil thoroughly. In a pan put all the masalas (whole), a little oil and the turmeric and chilli powders and salt. Put in the mango pieces and coat them well with this masala. Put in a clean jar and keep for 2 days in the sun, shaking occasionally. Pour oil on the third day and keep in a dry cool place. Lasts for a year or more.

Note : (This is for a Tropical Climate). In a dry climate the mangoes can be cut, all the masalas added and oil mixed at the same time).

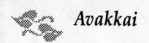

Avakkai

$2\frac{1}{2}$ kg hard, green mangoes
$1\frac{1}{4}$ cups mustard seed powder
$1\frac{1}{4}$ cups chilli powder
$1\frac{1}{2}$ cups salt
1 tbsp fenugreek seed powder
3 tbsp garlic cloves peeled
3 tbsp turmeric powder
$1\frac{1}{2}$ ltrs gingelly oil

Wash and dry mangoes. Cut them right through the cores. Remove cores and cut again in 2 cm cubes.

In a big basin add all the powdered masalas, salt, garlic cloves and half the oil. Mix well with hand adding the cut mangoes. Mix till pieces are well coated. Put in a big jar, tie a clean cloth on top and sun it for three days. Shake well every day and pour the rest of the oil on the pickle to cover it 2 cm above top level.

Can be kept for a year.

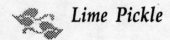

Mango Kutra

2 kg green mangoes—peel and cut in thin strips

Broil and pound
3 tbsp aniseeds
1¹/₂ tbsp fenugreek seeds
1 tbsp nigella seeds

2 tbsp chilli powder
2 tbsp turmeric powder
2 tbsp mustard seed powder
1 kg oil (mustard, groundnut or gingelly)
salt to taste

Heat oil, take off the fire, add pounded masalas and let fry. When cool add chilli, turmeric and mustard seed powders and the salt. Add mango strips. Mix well. Cool, bottle and preserve.

Lime Pickle

50 limes

Broil separately and powder
50 red chillies
2 tbsp fenugreek seeds
12 tbsp mustard seeds
pea size piece asafoetida

2 tbsp turmeric powder
1¹/₄ cups salt

Wash and dry the limes and cut into 8 pieces each. Mix broiled powders, turmeric and salt, add these to cut limes and mix well with hand to coat all the pieces.

Fill in jar, tie with a cloth and sun for 7-10 days. Shake every day. Can be kept for a year.

Whole Limes in Salt

50 kagzi limes
$^3/_4$ kg salt

Rub each lime well on coarse stone or grater, to remove oil. Cut into fours halfway down without separating. Fill each with salt and place in a jar.

Add more salt and shake well. Place in the sun for a month till the lemons swell and juice jells (shake every day without fail). It can be kept for years.

Lemon Pickle

2 kg lemons—wash, wipe and slit in quarters
    without separating pieces
1 kg lemons—squeeze out juice

Powder
150 gms sugar
250 gms black salt
25 gms big black cardamoms
15 gms peppercorns
25 gms red chillies
15 gms cumin seeds
15 gms black cumin seeds
15 gms carom seeds
pea size piece asafoetida
100 gms dried ginger

Take ¼ cup lemon juice and mix the powders in it. Stuff the cut lemons with the masala mixture. Arrange in glass jars with layers of masala between lemons. Pour remaining lemon juice. Cover and sun for two weeks, shaking occasionally.

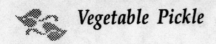

Vegetable Pickle

1 kg mixed vegetables (carrots, knol khol, brinjals)
100 gms garlic ground
$^{1}/_{2}$ kg mustard or gingelly oil

Soak in 2 cups vinegar overnight
100 gms dry dates
100 gms raisins

Grind
50 gms almonds blanched
100 gms mustard seeds
200 gms sugar
chilli powder and salt to taste
100 gms cumin seeds

Heat a little oil, fry vegetables slightly and remove. In the same oil fry garlic. Add ground masala and take it off the fire. Drain out soaked raisins and dates and mix in. Heat the rest of the oil till smoking. Cool and add to vegetables. Bottle when cool.

Mixed Vegetable Pickle

2 kg turnips—peel and cut in rings
2 kg carrots—scrape and cut lengthwise
1 kg cauliflower—cut in flowerets
1½ kg mustard oil

Grind
250 gms garlic
750 gms onions
200 gms ginger

3 tbsp red chilli powder
3 tbsp turmeric powder
1 tbsp garam masala
175 gms mustard seeds

Cook into a syrup
1½ bottles vinegar
1 kg jaggery

salt to taste
1 stick ratan jot or ½ pkt degi mirch

Heat oil, fry 'ratan jot' and discard it. In the same oil fry ground masala. Take off the fire. Add the powder masalas, salt and vegetables. Keep on the fire again and cook for another 5 minutes, very briskly. Add syrup and take off the fire. Cool thoroughly before bottling.

Tamarind Pickle

1 kg tamarind
1¹/₂ kg jaggery
salt to taste

Broil and powder fine
3 tbsp cumin seeds
16 red chillies

Broil and pound a little
3 tbsp aniseeds
2 tsp fenugreek seeds
2 tsp nigella seeds
1¹/₂ tsp carom seeds

Soak tamarind in 2 cups water. Mash well and force through a strainer, with hands, to get the maximum pulp. Discard seeds and strings. Boil jaggery in a cup of water and strain through muslin cloth to remove any impurities. Mix the jaggery and tamarind juice and keep on fire and boil till liquid is reduced to half. Add salt and chilli-cumin seed powder and cook till thick. Add broiled and pounded masalas. Cook for one minute more. Take off the fire, cool and bottle.

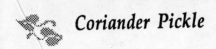

Coriander Pickle

4 cups coriander leaves dried in the sun for a day
$1^1/_2$ tsp fenugreek seeds—roast and powder
2 tsp mustard seed powder
little asafoetida
1 tbsp chilli powder
$^1/_2$ tsp mustard seeds
$^1/_2$ tsp cumin seeds
$1^1/_2$ cups gingelly oil
1 cup vinegar
salt to taste

Heat oil, add asafoetida and splutter mustard and cumin seeds. Add chilli, mustard and fenugreek powders and the coriander leaves. Let cook for 2-3 minutes and add salt and vinegar. Cook till oil separates. Cool and bottle.

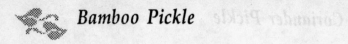

Bamboo Pickle

750 gms tender bamboo shoots cut in thin slices
4 cups vinegar
1¹/₂ tbsp salt
250 gms sugar
12 allspice
1 pod garlic—peel and keep cloves
12 red chillies—punch
5 cm piece ginger cut in strips

Soak bamboo slices overnight in cold water. Drain water. Add a cup of fresh water and boil for 20 minutes. Strain and let them dry thoroughly with cloth or under the fan for ½ an hour.

Boil vinegar, allspice, sugar and salt. Drain and keep the syrup aside. To the syrup, add garlic, ginger, chillies and bamboo shoots and cook on slow fire for 20 minutes. Bottle when cool.

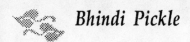

Bhindi Pickle

250 gms tender lady's fingers
100 gms green chillies sliced
100 gms ginger shredded
30 gms slaked lime
20 lemons—extract juice

Mix together
100 gms mustard seed powder
100 gms salt
50 gms turmeric powder

Soak whole lady's fingers in lime water for 10 minutes. Drain and wipe each one well. Slit lady's fingers lengthwise and stuff each one with masala. Arrange in layers of lady's finger, ginger and chillies in a jar. Tie the mouth of the jar with muslin cloth and sun it for 4 days. Pour lime juice on the 5th day and sun it again for a week, shaking the jar every day.

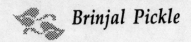

Brinjal Pickle

Grind to a fine paste with a little vinegar
30 gms red chillies
90 gms mustard seeds
90 gms cumin seeds
10 cm piece ginger
6 pods garlic

2 500 ml bottles vinegar
1 kg groundnut or gingelly oil
2 tsp mustard seeds
1 tsp fenugreek seeds
5 cm piece ginger cut in strips
1 pod garlic cut in small pieces
1 tsp cumin seeds
a sprig curry leaves
1¹/₂ kg long brinjals cut in small pieces
salt to taste
2 tbsp turmeric powder
3 tbsp sugar

Heat oil, splutter mustard, fenugreek and cumin seeds, add ginger, garlic and curry leaves and fry. Add ground masala and fry well. Add turmeric, salt, brinjal pieces, rest of the vinegar and sugar till brinjals are well cooked and oil separates. Cool and fill in bottles.

Note : Cut brinjals when masala is frying to avoid discolouration.

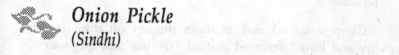

Cucumber Pickle

1 kg tender, equal size cucumbers
2 tbsp salt
1 cup sugar
1 bottle vinegar
10 red chillies
12 peppercorns

Peel and cut cucumbers in halves, remove seeds and pith, prick with fork, sprinkle with salt and let drain in the sun for a day. Make syrup with sugar and vinegar, adding whole chillies and peppercorns. Wipe cucumbers dry and give one gentle boil in syrup, adding a little more salt. Cool and bottle.

Onion Pickle
(Sindhi)

1 kg button onions
3 tbsp Banarsi rai—powder not too fine
1 tsp turmeric powder
1 tbsp chilli powder
salt to taste
2 cups water

Peel onions and mix with powders. Add salt, and water and sun them for 3-4 days. Will be ready on 5th day.

Cannot be kept more than 10 days.

Variation: 1 kg carrots. Peel and cut into fours. Give one gentle boil. Strain. Cool and follow the same procedure as above, substituting 1 tbsp oil for 2 cups water.

Mix and keep. It will be ready in 6 days time.

Keeps only for 3-4 weeks.

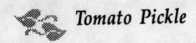

Tomato Pickle

5 kg ripe and firm tomatoes

Powder
250 gms mustard seeds
250 gms cumin seeds
250 gms red chillies
100 gms turmeric
50 gms fenugreek seeds

Grind to a paste
300 gms garlic
300 gms ginger

salt to taste
1¹/₂ 500 ml bottles vinegar or
4 tbsp acetic acid
1¹/₂ kg gingelly or groundnut oil
¹/₂ tsp asafoetida

Chop tomatoes and let them simmer on slow fire till pulpy and liquid reduced to half. (Do not add any water). Heat oil, fry asafoetida and crush it, add ground paste and fry till golden brown. Add tomato pulp and the powders and cook on fire, stirring all the time. Add vinegar (or acetic acid) and salt when half-cooked. Cook till oil separates. Cool and fill bottles.

Turnip Pickle

$1^1/_2$ kg white turnips peeled and cut in rings
20 gms turmeric powder
30 gms red chillies
$^1/_2$ cup vinegar
$1^1/_2$ bottles mustard oil
40 gms ginger
30 gms garlic
$2^1/_2$ tbsp salt
12 green chillies

Roast and pound
30 gms cumin seeds
30 gms fenugreek seeds
30 gms mustard seeds

Mix together
$^1/_2$ kg jaggery
3 cups vinegar

Grind the turmeric, red chillies, half the ginger and half the garlic in ½ cup vinegar. Bring oil to boil and add the ground ingredients. Remove from fire and add cut turnip rings and fry for one or two minutes. Add remaining garlic and ginger cut in strips, salt and green chillies. Cook until the vegetable is half cooked. Add jaggery and vinegar liquid and the masala powder. Cook till vegetable is nearly tender.

Cool and fill in clean jars.

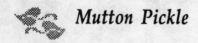

Mutton Pickle

1 kg mutton cut in 2 cm cubes
$\frac{1}{2}$ kg mustard oil
1 tbsp turmeric powder
salt to taste
2 cups vinegar

Grind
6 dry, red chillies
16 cloves garlic
7 cm piece ginger

Powder
7 cm stick cinnamon
10 cardamoms
10 cloves
1 tbsp peppercorns

Heat oil in a pan, fry the cubes of mutton till brown.
Remove and to the same oil add ground paste and brown.
Add powdered masala, turmeric, salt and mutton pieces.
Cook for 3 minutes. Pour vinegar and cook on very slow fire
till oil separates. Cool and preserve in glass jars.

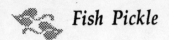

Fish Pickle

1 kg fish—cut in 5 cm pieces
1 tsp salt
$^1/_2$ tsp chilli powder
$^1/_2$ tsp turmeric powder
oil for frying
12 peppercorns
12 allspice
1 500 ml bottle vinegar
salt to taste
6 red chillies

Grind
2 cm piece ginger
12 cloves garlic

Apply salt, turmeric and chilli powders to fish pieces. Keep for 30-40 minutes. Heat oil, fry fish golden brown, drain and keep aside. Boil vinegar adding chillies, peppercorns, allspice, ground masala and salt. Place fish pieces in a wide mouthed jar and pour vinegar to cover fish pieces. Cool and preserve.

Prawn Pickle

150 gms cleaned prawns
$^1/_2$ cup gingelly oil
1 gm asafoetida powder
15 gms fenugreek seed powder
75 gms red chilli powder
30 gms mustard seed powder
15 gms turmeric powder
75 gms salt
1 cup vinegar

Heat oil, fry asafoetida, add prawns and salt. Cover and cook till prawns are soft. Reduce heat, add the other powders and fry for another 5 minutes. Cool and put in a jar. Next day add vinegar.

Burmese Balachow I

1 kg shelled prawns—soak overnight and grind
3 shoots lemon grass or a sprig curry leaves
1 cup tamarind juice
salt to taste
1 500 ml bottle gingelly oil
1 dsp nypai dried fish powder

Powder
2 tsp cumin seeds
1 tsp peppercorns
1 tbsp turmeric powder
16 red chillies

Grind to a paste
3 onions
6 pods garlic
7 cm piece ginger

Heat oil thoroughly, add ground paste of onions, garlic, ginger and lemon grass. Fry till golden in colour, add prawn paste and the powders. Cook for 6-8 minutes. Add tamarind juice and salt and cook till juice is absorbed and the oil floats on top. Cool and bottle.

Nypayi can be added before adding the tamarind juice.

Burmese Balachow II

3 cups dried prawns
2 onions
1 pod garlic
2 cm piece ginger
20 red chillies
1 cup vinegar
3 shoots lemon grass

Chop and fry crisp
2 oinons
1 tbsp garlic

1 cup gingelly oil
salt to taste
1 cup tamarind juice

Pick prawns. Wash and soak till soft. Grind prawns in vinegar. Grind red chillies and all the other ingredients together except tamarind juice and salt.

Heat oil, fry chilli paste till brown. Add prawn paste, tamarind juice and salt. Cook till juice is absorbed and oil separates and floats on top. Bottle when cool.

Dried Prawns

250 gms fresh prawns after cleaning
1 tbsp salt
½ tsp turmeric powder

Shell and devein prawns, keep in salt and turmeric solution for a day. String and dry in the sun (15-20 days). Bottle and keep.

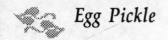

Egg Pickle

12 eggs—boil and shell
1 pod garlic—peel and mince
2 cm piece ginger—peel and mince
16 peppercorns
16 allspice
1 tbsp sugar
salt to taste
1 750 ml bottle vinegar

Boil vinegar alongwith all other ingredients except eggs.
Place cooled eggs in a jar and pour spiced vinegar on top.
Bottle and keep. Will be ready in a fortnight.

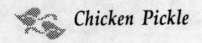

Chicken Pickle

1 small chicken cleaned and jointed

Grind to a fine paste with vinegar
12 red chillies
120 gms cumin seeds
10 pods garlic
7 cm piece ginger

1 500 ml bottle vinegar
1 500 ml bottle gingelly oil
salt to taste

Heat oil, fry chicken pieces till golden brown. Remove and fry the ground masala in the same oil. Add chicken pieces and the remaining vinegar and salt. Cook for another 10 minutes on slow fire. Cool and fill in jars.

Variation : Boil chicken pieces in vinegar instead of frying. Fry the paste in oil, add boiled chicken pieces and vinegar mixed with 200 gms of jaggery. Cook until gravy is thick. Cool and fill in jars.

CHUTNEYS

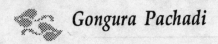

Gongura Pachadi

$^1/_4$ kg gongura/tainga saag
4 green chillies
1 tsp turmeric powder
$^1/_4$ kg oil
small piece asafoetida
25 dry, red chillies
1 tsp fenugreek seeds
salt to taste

Pluck saag leaves. Fry saag and green chillies in oil, adding turmeric powder, till pulpy. Heat little of the oil, fry asafoetida, dry chillies and fenugreek seeds. Pound well and powder. Add to saag and grind adding salt to taste.

Keeps only a few weeks.

Cheena Badam Chutney

Grind to a paste
1 cup roasted, husked groundnuts
$^1/_2$ dry coconut (copra)
2-3 green chillies
salt to taste

1 cup curd
2 tsp oil
$^1/_2$ tsp mustard seeds
a sprig curry leaves

Add all the ground ingredients to whipped curd. In a pan, heat oil, splutter mustard seeds, curry leaves and pour over chutney and mix.

Goes well with idli, dosa and pakoras.

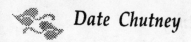

Date Chutney

Grind to a paste
100 gms dates stoned
100 gms raisins
8 red chillies
5 cm piece ginger
1 pod garlic

75 gms sugar
1 tsp salt
2 cups vinegar

In a thick bottomed pan mix sugar, vinegar, salt and heat till sugar is dissolved. Add ground paste and cook till liquid evaporates. Cool and fill in sterilised jars.

Date and Raisin Chutney

$^1/_2$ kg dates—stone, soak and cut in strips
100 gms raisins—wash, soak and drain
250 gms jaggery
3 balls tamarind (lemon size)
salt to taste
1 tsp chilli powder
$1^1/_2$ tbsp roasted cumin seed powder
2 cups water
1 tsp ginger powder

In 2 cups water soak tamarind and jaggery for half an hour. Mash well and strain, removing all the liquid and pulp. Add salt, roasted and powdered cumin seeds and chilli and ginger powders. Mix well, add dates and drained raisins.

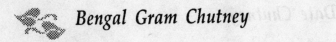

Bengal Gram Chutney

1 coconut grated
1 lemon size ball tamarind
$^1/_2$ tsp nigella seeds
1 sprig curry leaves
1 tbsp oil
salt to taste

Fry in very little oil
6 tbsp Bengal gram dal
5 red chillies

Grind to a paste, fried dal, chillies, grated coconut and tamarind. Add salt. Heat 1 tbsp oil, splutter nigella and curry leaves and pour on chutney. Add a little buttermilk if you want the chutney to be of thin consistency.

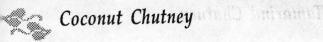

Coconut Chutney

Grind to a fine paste
1 coconut grated
6 tbsp Bengal gram—soak for $\frac{1}{2}$ an hr
5 red chillies
1 cm piece ginger
lemon size ball tamarind

1 tbsp oil
$\frac{1}{2}$ tsp mustard seeds
2 red chillies broken into small pieces
few curry leaves
salt to taste

Heat oil, splutter mustard seeds and chillies. Add curry leaves, ground paste and salt. Mix well. Add half a cup of water and cook for 5 minutes. Cool and serve.

Variation : Instead of adding water and cooking for 5 minutes add half cup buttermilk, mix and serve.

Tamarind Chutney

$^1/_2$ kg fresh tamarind—shell and remove seeds
1 tsp turmeric powder
salt to taste
$1^1/_2$ cups refined oil
a pinch asafoetida
1 tsp mustard seeds
$^1/_2$ tsp fenugreek seeds
1 tsp urad dal
100 gms red chillies—fry and pound
30 gms jaggery
3-4 green chillies
1 tbsp coriander leaves

Heat oil, fry asafoetida, dal, mustard and fenugreek seeds and pound. Grind jaggery along with the tamarind and chillies finely. Add turmeric powder and salt. (After adding masala do not grind much).

If the chutney is to be kept for a long time the green chillies and coriander leaves should not be added. This tamarind pounded with turmeric and salt can be kept for more than a year. Whenever necessary, take a little of it, fry the required ingredients and make the chutney adding the green chillies and coriander leaves for extra flavour.

Tamarind-Ginger Chutney

1 kg seedless, dry tamarind
$^1/_4$ kg garlic—peel
$^1/_4$ kg ginger—peel
350 gms jaggery
salt to taste
1 tbsp turmeric powder
$^1/_2$ kg red chillies
$^1/_2$ kg oil
3 tbsp Bengal gram dal
3 tbsp black gram dal
$1^1/_2$ tbsp mustard seeds
1 sprig curry leaves
8 dry, red chillies
2 pods garlic peeled and chopped fine

Put tamarind in a pan and pour enough cold water to cover it fully. Keep for an hour. Mash and grind well with garlic, ginger, jaggery and turmeric powder. In a little oil fry the red chillies and powder them. Add to ground tamarind and grind again adding salt till it becomes one. Heat oil, add chopped garlic, Bengal gram, black gram, mustard seeds, curry leaves, broken chillies and pour over the tamarind. Cool and preserve. Can be kept for a year or more.

Ripe Banana Chutney

Boil and strain
250 gms tamarind
300 gms jaggery
2 cups water

4 ripe, firm bananas
1 tsp ginger powder
1 tbsp roasted coriander seed powder
1 tsp black salt
$^{1}/_{2}$ tsp garam masala
1 tsp chilli powder
salt to taste
100 gms raisins soaked and drained

To strained juice add all the ingredients and boil till reduced to half the quantity. Cool. Cut bananas into thick slices and add to cooled liquid. Serve cold.

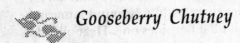

Gooseberry Chutney

1 kg gooseberries—remove stems and blossom ends
750 gms sugar
1 cup water
250 gms raisins—pick, wash and soak in vinegar
150 gms dates—soak in vinegar, stone and chop

Grind in vinegar
5 cm piece ginger
20 cloves garlic
15 red chillies

1 750 ml bottle vinegar
salt to taste

Cook gooseberries, sugar and water for 20 minutes. Add the rest of the ingredients and the remaining vinegar and simmer to a thick consistency. Cool and bottle.

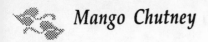

Mango Chutney

1 kg mangoes (mature but not ripe)
1$^1/_2$ tbsp salt

Make syrup
$^1/_2$ kg sugar
1$^1/_2$ cups vinegar

1 pod garlic—peel cloves and keep whole
12 peppercorns
$^1/_2$ ball tamarind (size of lemon)
1 tsp chilli powder
1 tsp garam masala

Pound coarse
1 tbsp cumin seeds
$^1/_2$ tbsp fenugreek seeds

Cut mangoes in strips, apply salt and marinate for one hour. Add mangoes to syrup along with garlic cloves and cook. When half done add all the other ingredients and cook on very slow fire (with a heavy weight on top of the lid) for 30-40 minutes. Cool and bottle.

Mango Kasaundi

Sun for 4 days and let brine drip
2 kg raw mangoes—peel and slice very fine
2¹/₂ tbsp salt

Grind using a little vinegar
10 red chillies
2 tbsp turmeric powder
100 gms mustard seeds
100 gms cumin seeds
100 gms fenugreek seeds

2 tbsp ginger slices
1 tbsp garlic slices
2 cups jaggery
1 750 ml bottle vinegar
2 lemon size balls tamarind
2 cups gingelly or groundnut oil
salt to taste

In 1 cup vinegar soak tamarind for 1 hour. Mash well and strain the pulp out. Throw seeds and residue. Soak jaggery in 1 cup vinegar and mix well.

Heat oil, fry garlic, ginger slices a little, add ground ingredients and fry for a while. Add mango pieces, jaggery, tamarind and remaining vinegar and cook for 15 minutes till well blended. Cool and bottle.

Note : Taste and add salt, if needed, before cooking for 15 minutes.

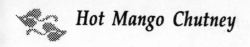

Hot Mango Chutney

12 green mangoes (mature but not ripe)

Broil and powder
20 red chillies
2 tsp fenugreek seeds

$^1/_2$ tsp asafoetida—fry in a little oil and powder
$1^1/_2$ tbsp mustard seeds
2 tsp turmeric powder
salt to taste
$^1/_4$ kg oil

Peel and grate mangoes. Heat oil, splutter mustard seeds, add grated mangoes, turmeric and salt. Stir well and cook till most of the liquid evaporates and oil separates. Add chilli, fenugreek and asafoetida powders. Mix well. Cool and bottle.

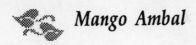

Mango Ambal

10 raw mangoes—roast on fire and squeeze out pulp

Broil and make panch phoran powder
$^1/_2$ tsp aniseeds
$^1/_2$ tsp fenugreek seeds
$^1/_2$ tsp mustard seeds
$^1/_2$ tsp cumin seeds
$^1/_2$ tsp nigella seeds

1 tbsp mustard oil
$^1/_2$ tsp mustard seeds
2 tbsp sugar
salt to taste
1 cup water

Heat oil, splutter mustard seeds, add mango pulp, sugar, salt and water. Cook till gravy is thick. Add panch phoran powder and serve.

Variation : Chop mangoes in small pieces and add 2 cups water instead of one and follow the same procedure as above.

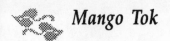

Mango Tok

6 tart, green mangoes
1 tbsp oil
1 tsp panch phoran
2 red chillies broken
1½ tbsp poppy seeds—wash and grind to a fine paste
4 tbsp sugar
salt to taste
1½ cups water

Peel and grate mangoes. Mix poppy seed paste with one cup of water, strain and keep the liquid.

Heat 1 tbsp oil till smoking hot. Splutter panch phoran and red chillies. Add grated mangoes, salt and poppy seed liquid and cook till mango pieces are soft. Add sugar and boil for another 5 minutes. (There should be enough liquid left over after cooking).

Sweet Lime Chutney

Fill with salt and sun for 3 days
12 limes cut in quarters
1 tbsp salt

1 500 ml bottle vinegar
150 gms raisins
1 tbsp ginger
1 tbsp garlic
1 tsp red chilli powder
1 tsp mustard seeds broiled, husked
120 gms sugar

Discard seeds from dried limes. Grind them with a cupful of vinegar and all the other ingredients except sugar, to a fine paste. Add the rest of the vinegar and sugar and cook for 45-50 minutes on a very slow fire stirring occasionally.

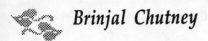

Brinjal Chutney

6 long brinjals—roast on hot ashes or in hot oven
1 tsp oil
3 red chillies
2 tbsp Bengal gram—soak for 20 mins
1 pinch asafoetida
salt to taste

Strain pulp
1 lemon size ball tamarind
$1/_4$ cup water

Remove skins from roasted brinjals. Remove stems and seeds. Mash and mix with tamarind pulp. Heat ghee, add asafoetida, fry broken red chillies and drained gram dal. Take off the fire and grind to a smooth paste. Add to brinjal-tamarind mash and mix salt.

Cucumber Chutney

2 big cucumbers
2 tsp salt
3 tbsp roasted peanuts powdered
1 tsp sugar
1 tbsp lemon juice
2 green chillies
1 tbsp oil
1 pinch asafoetida
$1/4$ tsp mustard seeds
$1/2$ tsp cumin seeds
a few curry leaves

Peel, seed and cut cucumbers in very fine cubes. Salt and marinate for half an hour. Squeeze out water and add peanut powder, sliced green chillies, sugar, lemon juice and mix well. Heat oil, splutter asafoetida, mustard and cumin seeds. Add curry leaves and add to cucumber mixture.

Green Chilli Chutney

$^1/_2$ cup gingelly oil
pea size asafoetida
$^1/_2$ tsp fenugreek seeds
4 tsp mustard seeds
100 gms green chillies—slit and remove tails

Mix
1 cup tamarind juice
1 tbsp jaggery
1 tsp turmeric powder
1 tbsp salt or to taste

Heat oil, fry asafoetida and mash it up, splutter fenugreek and mustard seeds. Add chillies and fry them well. Pour tamarind mixture and cook again till oil floats on top. Cool and bottle.

Mint Chutney

1 bunch mint leaves
$^1/_2$ bunch coriander leaves
4 spring onions
1 pod garlic
8 green chillies
1 tbsp pomegranate seeds
salt to taste

Pluck mint leaves and grind all the ingredients together to a very fine paste.

Note: If pomegranate seeds are not available tamarind can be used.

Onion Chutney

Grind to a paste
4 large onions—peel and chop
1 bunch coriander leaves
1 tsp mint leaves chopped
1 tbsp pomegranate seeds or mango powder
6 green chillies
$^1/_2$ cup peanuts roasted
2 cm piece ginger

salt to taste
1 tsp oil
$^1/_4$ tsp mustard seeds
1 tsp urad dal
a few curry leaves
2 tbsp tamarind juice

Heat oil, splutter mustard seeds, add urad dal and curry leaves. Add to ground paste, mix salt and lastly add tamarind juice and serve.

Tomato Chutney

4 kg ripe, firm tomatoes

Make syrup
1 750 ml bottle vinegar
1$\frac{1}{2}$ kg sugar

Pound a little but do not powder
2 tsp aniseeds
2 tsp fenugreek seeds
1 tsp nigella seeds

4 bay leaves
1 nutmeg grated
3 blades mace crushed
2 tsp chilli powder
10 whole, red chillies seeded
salt to taste

Chop tomatoes, add to syrup and cook till reduced to half. Add seeded red chillies and all the other ingredients and cook till thickish, adding salt lastly. Cook another few minutes. Cool and bottle.

Tomato Tok

1 kg ripe tomatoes chopped
2 cm piece ginger—chopped fine
100 gms raisins
1 tsp mustard seeds or panch phoran
3 whole, red chillies
1 cup sugar
salt to taste
1 tbsp ghee
2 cups water

Cook tomatoes on very slow fire till soft and pulpy. Heat ghee, fry ginger and raisins, splutter mustard seeds or panch phoran and chillies. Add tomato pulp, sugar and salt. Add 2 cups water and cook till well done and a cupful liquid remains.

Green Tomato and Apple Chutney

1 kg green tomatoes
120 gms onions
2 cooking apples
60 gms sultanas
50 gms raisins

Make a bouquet garni
10 peppercorns
10 allspice
1 tsp mustard seeds

salt to taste
1 500 ml bottle vinegar
200 gms sugar

Put tomatoes in boiling water for a minute. Strain and peel skins. Skin and core apples and mince along with tomatoes, onions, sultanas and raisins. Add to vinegar along with the bouquet garni, and simmer for half an hour. Remove bouquet garni add sugar and stir until it is dissolved. Add salt and cook for another 45-50 minutes.

Sweet Tomato Chutney

2¹/₂ kg firm, ripe tomatoes
2¹/₂ kg sugar
120 gms salt
2 500 ml bottles vinegar

Make a bouquet garni
10 allspice berries
10 peppercorns
4 black cardamoms
8 cloves
2 bay leaves
1 tsp cumin seeds
6 whole, red chillies
2 onions chopped
1 pod garlic chopped
5 cm piece ginger

Chop tomatoes, simmer till soft and pulpy, strain the pulp and discard skins and seeds. To the pulp add sugar, salt and bouquet garni. Cook for half an hour. Remove bouquet garni, add vinegar and cook again to a thick consistency.

Keeps indefinitely.

Tomato-Onion-Mint Chutney

2 onions chopped very fine
3 firm, ripe tomatoes chopped

Grind to a paste
1 tbsp mint leaves
1 tbsp coriander leaves
6 green chillies
2 cm piece ginger

2 tsp cumin seeds broiled and powdered
$^1/_2$ tsp chilli powder
2 cups curd
salt to taste

Beat curd well, add ground paste, chopped onions, tomatoes and salt. Mix well and cool in refrigerator. Before serving, garnish with cumin seed and chilli powders.

Glossary

English	Hindi
Acetic acid	Sirka
Acorn	Thuja/majuphal
African cucumber	Karela
Agar-agar	China grass
Alkali	Sajji/khar
Allspice/pimento	Kababchini
Almonds	Badaam
Aloe	Mussabar
Alum	Phitkari
Amaranth	Chaulai
Ammonium chloride	Naushadar
Aniseed	Saunf
Apricot	Khurmani
Areca-nut	Supari
Artichoke	Hathichuk
Arum	Kachchu
Asafoetida	Hing
Ash gourd	Petha
Aubergine	Baingan
Bamboo	Baans
Bamboo shoots	Baans ki koplain
Banyan	Bar
Barley	Jau
Basil leaves	Tulasi ke patte
Bautini	Kachnaar
Bay leaf	Tejpatta

English	Hindi
Beans	
Cluster	Guar phalli
Cowgram	Lobia
French	Frash been
Hyacinth	Sem
Sword	Bari sem
Beaten rice	Chivda/chidwa
Beetroot	Chukandar
Bengal gram	Chana
Betel leaf	Paan-patta
Betel nut	Supari
Bishop's weed	Ajwain
Bitter gourd	Karela
Black salt	Kala namak
Borax	Suhaga
Bottle gourd	Lauki
Bouquet garni	Masalae-ki-potli
Bran	Chokkar
Brinjal	Baingan
Brown sugar	Shakkar
Bullock's heart	Ramphal
Butter	Makhan
Butter-milk	Mattha
Cabbage	Band gobi
Camphor	Kapoor
Cape gooseberry	Rasbhari
Capsicum	Shimla mirch
Carambola	Kamrakh
Caraway seeds	Shahjeera
Cardamoms (black)	Motti elaichi
Cardamoms (green)	Chhotti elaichi
Carom seeds	Ajwain
Carrisa carandas	Karonda
Carrots	Gajjar
Cashewnuts	Kaju
Cassia leaves	Tejpatta
Castor oil	Arendi ka tael
Castor seeds	Arendi

English	Hindi
Catechu	Kattha
Cauliflower	Phool gobi
Celery	Ajmude
Cherry	Glas
Chilli powder	Pissi lal mirch
Cinnamon	Dalchini
Citric acid	Nimbu satt
Clarified butter	Ghee
Cloves	Laung/lavang
Cochineal	Lal rang
Coconut	Nariyal
Colocasia	Arbi
Colocasia leaves	Arbi ke pattae
Condiments	Masalae
Copper sulphate	Neela thotha
Copra	Sookha nariyal
Coriander leaves	Hara dhania/kothmir
Coriander powder	Pissa dhania
Coriander seeds	Sookha sabut dhania
Corn cob	Bhutta
Cottage cheese	Dahi ka paneer
Cotton seeds	Binaulae
Crab	Kekra
Cream	Malai
Cress	Halim
Cubeb	Kababchini
Cucumber	Kheera
Cumin seed powder	Pissa zeera
Cumin seeds	Zeera
Curd	Dahi
Currants	Daakh
Curry leaves	Gandhela/curry patta
Custard apple	Sharifa
Cutch	Kattha
Cuttle bone	Samundar jhaag
Dates	Khajoor
Dill	Soya
Dried apricots	Khurmani/jardalu

English	Hindi
Drumsticks	Suanjana ki phalli
Dry ginger	Sonth
Egg-plant	Baingan
Elephant's foot	Zimikand/suren
Essence	Satt
Fennel	Bari saunf
Fenugreek leaves	Methi saag
Fenugreek seeds	Methae
Figs	Anjeer
Flea seeds	Isabgol
Foxnuts	Makhanae
Fumet	Fish stock
Garcinia indica	Cocum
Garlic	Lahsun
Gelatine	Saresh
Gingelly oil	Til ka tael
Ginger (fresh)	Adrak
Ginger (dry)	Sonth
Gooseberry	Rasbhari
Gourd (ash)	Petha
" (bitter)	Karela
" (bottle)	Lauki
" (pointed)	Parwal
" (red)	Lal kaddu
" (ridge)	Kali tori
" (snake)	Chachinda
" (sponge)	Ghiya tori
" (wax)	Petha
Gram	Chana
Gram flour	Besan
Grapes	Angoor/daakh
Gravy	Shorwa
Green chillies	Hari mirch
Greens	Saag
Groundnuts	Moongphalli
Gruel	Maand

English	Hindi
Gum (Arabic)	Babul
Hazelnut (Chinese)	Leechi
Hemp (Indian)	Bhang/ganja
Henna	Mehndi
Hog-plum	Aanvala
Horse gram	Kultha
Jackfruit	Kathal
Jaggery	Gur
Jamaica pepper	Allspice
Jaundice berry	Kashmal
Jujube	Ber
Khol rabi/knol khol	Gaanth gobi
Kidneys	Gurdae
Lady's fingers	Bhindi
Leek	Vilayati pyaz
Lemon	Nimbu
Lemon grass	Gandha trina
Lemon peel	Nimbu chilka
Lentils	Dalaen
Lettuce	Salad patta
Liquorice	Mulatthi
Liver	Kaleji/jigar
Lotus seeds (puffed)	Makhanae
Lotus stems	Bhein
Luffa ribbed	Jhinga tori
Lump sugar	Mishri
Mace	Javitri
Mackerel	Bangda
Maize	Makkai
Margosa	Neem
Marjoram	Ban tulasi
Millet	Bajra
Mince meat	Keema
Mint leaves	Pudine ke pattae
Mixed spice	Garam masala
Molasses	Sheera/raab
Morrel	Guchchi

English	Hindi
Mulberry	Shahtoot
Mushrooms	Dhingri/khumb/ kukurmutta
Musk	Kastoori
Musk melon	Kharbooza
Mustard seeds (small)	Rai
Mustard seeds (big)	Sarson
Myrobalan belaric	Bahera
" chebulic	Harad
" emblica	Aanvala
Myrtle	Mehndi
Nigella seeds	Kalonji
Nutmeg	Jaiphal
Oats	Jau
Okra	Bhindi
Omum seeds	Ajwain
Pandanus flower	Kewra
Papadum	Pappad
Papaya	Papita
Peach	Aadu
Peanuts	Moongphalli
Pears	Naashpaatti
Peppercorns	Sabut kali mirch
Periwinkle	Ratanjote
Pickle	Achaar
Pigeon pea	Arhar dal
Pignoli/pine fruit	Chilgoza
Pineapple	Annanaas
Pistachio	Pista
Plums (black)	Jamun
" (bokhara)	Alu bokhara
Pomegranate	Anaar
Poppy seeds	Khus-Khus/posto
Potassium nitrate	Shora
Potato	Alu
Potato (sweet)	Shakarkandi
Prawns	Jheenga

English	Hindi
Pulses	Dal
Pumpkin	Kaddu
Purging cassia	Amaltas
Quail	Bataer
Quince	Bael
Radish	Mooli
Raisins	Kishmish
Raw plantain	Kachcha kela
Red chilli	Lal mirch
Red ochre	Geru
Rind	Chilka
Rock salt	Sendha namak
Rose apple	Safed jamun
Rose water	Gulab jal or arak
Ruddle	Geru
Saffron	Kesar
Sage	Malanga
Sago	Sagoodana
Salammoniac	Naushadar
Salt-petre	Shora
Sapid nuts	Chironji
Sebestan plum	Lasoora
Semolina	Sooji
Snake gourd	Chachinda
Sesame oil	Til ka tael
Sesame seeds	Til
Shorghum	Bajri
Silver leaves	Varak
Soda bicarbonate	Meetha soda
Solidified milk	Khoya
Sour lime	Khatta nimbu
Soya bean	Bhatwans
Spinach	Palak ka saag
Spring chicken	Chooza
Spring onion	Hara pyaz
Stock	Yakhni
Suet	Churbee

English	Hindi
Sugar-candy	Mishri
Sultanas	Munakkae
Summer squash	Chappan kaddu
Sweet lime	Mosambi
Tamarind	Imli
Tangarine	Santara
Testes (goat's)	Kapoorae
Thymol	Ajwain
Tomato	Tamatar
Treacle	Raab
Trotters	Paayae
Turmeric	Haldi
Turnip	Shalgam
Vegetable marrow	Safed kaddu
Venison	Hiran ka gosht
Vermicelli	Saviyan
Vinegar	Sirka
Walnuts	Akhrote
Water chestnuts	Singharae
Watermelon	Tarbooz
Wax gourd	Petha
Whey	Lassi
Wood apple	Bael
Yam	Ratalu
Yeast	Khameer
Yoghurt	Curd

Common Cooking Terms

Aspic	Clean jelly made from the cooked juices of meat, chicken or fish.
Baking	Cooking by dry heat in an oven.
Barbecue	To roast either whole or cut pieces of any meat on direct heat on a spit or rack.
Basting	Pouring spoonfuls of melted fat over the surface of food being baked or roasted.
Batter	Mixing of flour with water or milk into a thin consistency.
Beating	An up and down motion with a fork or rotary beater to mix the food thoroughly and to introduce air.
Binding	Adding egg, cream or melted fat to a dry mixture to hold it together.
Blanching	Removing the outer skin by plunging in hot water and then in cold water e.g., blanching of almonds or tomatoes.
Blending	Mixing of two or more ingredients into a smooth paste.
Boiling	Cooking in liquid at a temperature of 100^0C.
Boning	Removing bones of meat, poultry or fish.
Bouquet-garni	A muslin bag with herbs and condiments in it, tied at the top and cooked along with the stews or soups to flavour them. The bag is removed before the food is served.
Braising	Browning meat or vegetables in a casserole in a small amount of fat and then cooking in a little liquid with a lid on top.

Bread	To cover with fresh or dry bread crumbs completely.
Brine	Salt and water solution used for pickling or preserving.
Browning	Searing the outer surface of meat to seal in the juices.
Brushing	Applying an even coating of milk, egg or butter on the surface of food to get a shiny top.
Caramalize	To cook sugar till it turns golden brown.
Casserole	A cooking pot, complete with lid, made of ovenproof glass, flame-proof earthen or metal-ware.
Chantilly	Semi-sweet whipped cream.
Chilling	Cooling food without freezing it in the refrigerator.
Chowder	A liquidy stew made out of fish.
Coddling	Cooking slowly in simmering water (mainly used for eggs).
Colander	Perforated metal or plastic basket used for draining liquid.
Combine	To mix the ingredients.
Conchiglie	Conch-shaped pasta.
Crack-fry	Frying in a little fat on a very high flame to seal the juices (mainly used in Chinese cooking).
Creaming	Mixing two or more ingredients with a wooden spoon or mixer, to make it soft and fluffy.
Crepe	Thin pancake.
Croquette	Cooked and mashed mince meat, fish or vegetables, moulded in small shapes, dipped in egg, rolled in bread crumbs and then deep-fried.
Croustade	Small pieces of bread shapes, crisp fried and filled with savoury mixture.
Croutons	Small pieces of bread toasted in an oven or fried and served with soup.
Cure	To preserve fish or meat by salting and drying.

Cutting in	Combining fat with dry ingredients, by blending them with two knives or fingertips.
Devilling	Preparing meat, poultry, fish or vegetables with highly seasoned ingredients for grilling, roasting or baking.
Dicing	Cutting in small pieces.
Dot	To place small blobs of fat over the surface of the food.
Dough	A mixture of flour, water or milk, which is firm enough to knead and form into shapes.
Drain	To remove liquid from solid food.
Dredge	To sprinkle flour or sugar on food.
Dress	(a) To arrange or garnish food.
	(b) To pluck, draw and truss a chicken, turkey or duck.
Dressing	A sauce used for pouring on salads before serving.
Dusting	Sprinkling lightly with salt, pepper or flour or sugar or spices.
Escalope	Thin slices of meat that are beaten flat with a wooden meat-bat and then shallow fried.
Fillets	Long, thin boneless strips of meat or fish.
Flake	Separate food gently with a fork (like flaking fish from bones).
Folding in	Mixing one ingredient into another using a spatula.
Force meat	It is a stuffing made out of bread, meat and rice to which butter is added together with herbs and seasoning and filled in the cavity of a chicken, duck, goose or turkey.
Fricassee	To braise small pieces of food in very little hot oil turning frequently and then stewed or baked in sauce or gravy.
Frost	To coat a cake with an icing of confectioner's sugar.
Frying	Cooking of food in plenty of fat.

Garnish	Decorating a dish with something that adds colour and flavour.
Glaze	A glossy finish given to food by brushing with jelly, egg, milk, or sugar syrup.
Goulash	Beef and onion stew with pepper and tomato as ingredients.
Grate	To rub against a grater to get thin shreds.
Gravy	The resultant liquid that is left after boiling solid foods.
Grilling	Cooking under high heat directly over an open flame.
Grind	To cut, crush or force food through a chopper, grinding stone or a mixie.
Hash	A dish made from leftover chopped meat, potatoes and vegetables combined and then fried together.
Hull	Remove green calxy from fruits like strawberries or raspberries.
Icing	Coating cakes with icing sugar.
Julienne	Vegetable cut in thin matchlike strips.
Karahi	A heavy iron pan for deep frying.
Knead	To work dough with hands, pressing, stretching and folding until it is smooth.
Lasagne	Wide ribbon-like noodles.
Macerate	To soften food by soaking in liquid.
Marinate	To coat or soak in a mixture of oil, vinegar, spices and herbs for a period of time. It helps infuse flavours or tenderise as in the case of meat, fish or poultry.
Melt	To heat and liquify.
Mince	To chop food very fine.
Offal	Edible internal organs of meat, game or poultry.
Panch-Phoran	A mixture of nigella seeds, mustard seeds, cumin seeds, fenugreek seeds and aniseed used in Bengali cooking.

Parboil	To partially boil food.
Parch	To brown by means of dry heat.
Pare	To peel the outer covering.
Poach	To cook egg by placing it without shell in boiling water.
Punch	A drink usually of wine or spirits, mixed with chopped fruit, fruit juices, water or milk, sugar and spice etc.
Puree	Raw or cooked food which is passed through a sieve.
Rasping	Very fine crumbs obtained by rubbing stale bread or cake, on the fine side of a grater.
Roast	To cook by dry heat in an oven or on an open flame.
Roe	Eggs of the male fish which are soft whereas eggs of the female fish are called hard-roe.
Roux	Mixture of fat and flour which after cooking is used as a base for savoury sauces.
Rub in	Flour and fat which are mixed together by rubbing with the fingertips to resemble fine bread-crumbs.
Saute	To fry food rapidly in hot fat and tossing and turning often to brown evenly.
Scald	To heat milk or cream to just below boiling point.
Scoring	Cutting gashes on the surface of food.
Sear	To brown the surface of the food at a very high temperature.
Seasoning	Herbs and condiments used to improve the taste and appearance of food.
Scramble	To cook while mixing.
Shirr	To bake eggs in cream, vegetables and puree.
Sift	To pass through a sieve.
Skewers	Long metal or wooden thick pins used to pierce meat or fish for keeping them in place during roasting.
Skillet	A heavy iron shallow frying pan.

Smoking	Curing food like ham or fish by exposing it to wood smoke for a long time.
Steaming	Cooking in a double boiler or in a basin standing in (but not covered by) boiling water.
Steeping	Soaking in liquid to remove an ingredient e.g., salt from preserved ham.
Stewing	Simmering of food, meat or fruits, in a small amount of liquid to soften it.
Stirring	Mixing in a circular motion.
Stock	Liquid in which meat, fish or chicken is cooked.
Tagliatelle	Thin flat egg noodles.
Tarka	To garnish food with herbs and condiments by frying in hot fat to enrich its taste and flavour.
Toast	To cook food over dry heat or under a grill to make it brown and crisp.
Trivet	The perforated plate used in a pressure cooker through which steam passes.
Truffle	Subterranean mushroom-like fungus used for seasoning dishes.
Truss	To fasten wings etc., of fowl with thread before roasting.
Tutti-Frutti	Candied mixed fruits added to ice cream.
Vermicelli	Very fine strands of pasta.
Vinaigrette	A mixture of oil, vinegar, salt and pepper.
Wafer	Thin biscuits made from rice flour and served with ice cream.
Whip	To beat rapidly with fork, mixer or egg beater to introduce air so that volume is increased.
Zest	Grated outer skin of citrus fruit which is used to flavour foods and liquids.

EVERYONE'S BOOK OF
CHILD CARE

| Fully Illustrated |

DR. RENU JOGI

The Book Covers

- ❏ Child Care
- ❏ Growth and Development
- ❏ Feeding of Infants
- ❏ Nutrition and Health
- ❏ Balanced Diet
- ❏ Play
- ❏ Toilet Training

- ❏ The Importance of Immunization
- ❏ Common Diseases of Childhood
- ❏ Few ABC's of First Aid
- ❏ Behaviour Problems
- ❏ Discipline and Punishment

Rs. 45/-

YOGA
FOR INTEGRAL HEALTH

| Fully Illustrated |

DR. (MS.) V. VARMA

A 9-week Easy to Manage Yoga Course

The Book Covers

- ❏ Yoga and the Indian Tradition
- ❏ Yoga in the Context of Health
- ❏ Yogic Practices, Yogic Postures & Concentration Practices
- ❏ Health Protection, Healing and Menstrual Problems
- ❏ Summary and Conclusion

Rs. 45/-

MISS BEATTY'S CHILDREN

PAMELA ROOKS

An extraordinary novel, now a major film, a rage
of the 24th International Film Festival, Delhi '93.

"... One of the most smooth, controlled and placid narratives that I have read
in a long time... its steadiness of voice and unvarying competence are almost
uncanny. In fact, it is one of the most unusual and special novels that I have
read in a long time."

——————— *SUNDAY* ———————

Rs. 95/-

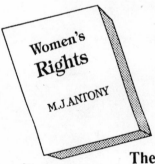

WOMEN'S RIGHTS

M. J. ANTONY

The Book Covers

- ❏ Constitution Protects Women
- ❏ Equal Pay
- ❏ Working Conditions
- ❏ Job Security
- ❏ Getting Married
- ❏ Defective Marriages
- ❏ Divorce without Bitterness
- ❏ Maintenance Tangle
- ❏ Crimes against Women
- ❏ Drawing up a Will

❏ Consumer Beware... and many more

Rs. 30/-